Y0-BPT-097

"ELINOR!" WAILED DORIS, "DID YOU HEAR THAT?"

A Little Maid
of
Maryland

BY

ALICE TURNER CURTIS

AUTHOR OF

A LITTLE MAID OF OLD CONNECTICUT
A LITTLE MAID OF MASSACHUSETTS COLONY
A LITTLE MAID OF OLD NEW YORK
A LITTLE MAID OF OLD PHILADELPHIA

ILLUSTRATED BY NAT LITTLE

APPLEWOOD BOOKS
BEDFORD, MASSACHUSETTS

A Little Maid of Maryland was first published by the Penn Publishing Company in 1923.

ISBN 1-55709-327-X

Thank you for purchasing an Applewood Book.
Applewood reprints America's lively classics—
books from the past that are still of interest to modern readers.
For a free copy of our current catalog, write to:
Applewood Books, Box 365, Bedford, MA, 01730.

10 9 8 7 6 5 4 3 2 1

Printed and bound in Canada.

Library of Congress Cataloging-in-Publication Data
Curtis, Alice Turner.
    A little maid of Maryland / by Alice Turner Curtis, author of
A little maid of old New York [and] A little maid of old
Philadelphia; illustrated by Nat Little.
    p.   cm.
    Summary: Living in Maryland during the time of the
colonies' rebellion against England, Barbara Anne accidentally
learns some secrets of the American patriots.
    ISBN 1-55709-327-X
    United States—History—Revolution, 1775–1783—Juvenile
fiction.   [1. United States—History—Revolution,
1775–1783—Fiction.   2. Maryland — History—Fiction.]   I.
Little, Nat, ill.   II. Title.

PZ7.C941Lmc   1996   95-49353
                                          CIP
                                          AC

Introduction

BARBARA ANNE was a little maid who lived in Maryland during the time of the Colonies' resistance to taxation by the mother country. While on a journey with her brother, she was lost, and blundered into a meeting of American patriots in the woods. She was branded by them as a spy, and not until she pledged never to speak of these men was she taken to her home. Although Barbara Anne met one of the men later, and was introduced to his crippled daughter, she always kept the secret deep down in her little heart. Through her efforts her brother, Oric, became an American patriot. By a trick she defeated the plans of a British officer and helped to carry important information to the general of the American forces.

CONTENTS

Illustrations

A Little Maid of Maryland

CHAPTER I

INTRODUCING BARBARA ANNE

"BARBARA ANNE! Barbara Anne! How do you suppose I can study, or think, or do *anything* with you making those barbarous noises? If you will try to sing don't stay on the terrace," called Doris Browne, leaning from an upper window of their father's big brick house, surrounded by fine gardens, that stood in the pleasant city of Annapolis, Maryland, overlooking the broad waters of Chesapeake Bay.

"One sang high, and one sang low,
  And the other sang bonny, bonny Biscay O!"

Barbara Anne sang valiantly at the top of her voice in response to her sister's complaint, and turned to look up defiantly at the window from which Doris had called.

But Doris had disappeared; and after repeating the song several times, Barbara Anne finally sauntered down the path to the lower garden feeling herself very much abused.

"It's just like Doris to say 'barbarous noises,'" she thought bitterly. "I s'pose she made up that word to fit my name, just because I'm the youngest. It's dreadful to be the youngest when there's five older children in the family," and Barbara Anne's face had a most serious expression as she recalled the fact that she had only just passed her eleventh birthday, while her sister Doris was thirteen, Elinor fifteen, and her three brothers "nearly grown up."

In fact Oric Browne, the eldest brother, had reached his twenty-first birthday and was employed as a secretary to Governor Eden who at that time, in the year 1774, was the governor of Maryland, appointed by England. Allen and Richard, who were respectively seventeen and nineteen, were their father's helpers and assistants in his ship-building yards that bordered on Annapolis harbor. Doris and Elinor felt themselves so much older than their little sister that Barbara Anne sometimes thought that they entirely forgot her existence.

"Doris and Elinor think that all I want is to play dolls," Barbara Anne reflected a little scornfully. "And as far as singing goes, I can sing as well as either of them!" And, as if to prove it, she again loudly repeated:

"One sang high, and one sang low,
  And the other sang bonny, bonny Biscay O!"

"Good for you, Bab! Want to go for a ride with me?" sounded a friendly, laughing voice from the other side of the thick hedge that shut the garden from the highway.

Barbara smiled happily at the sound of Allen's voice, and ran toward a tall iron gate that opened into the road.

"Yes, Allen, of course I do! Where are you going?" she called, even before she saw her brother who, mounted on a fine bay horse, was just beyond the entrance.

He smiled down at his little sister, whose brown curls were dancing about her face and whose brown eyes shone with delight at the happy prospect of a ride with Allen.

The young man swung himself from the saddle and lifted Barbara Anne to the horse's back, then reseated himself, and telling Barbara to "hold tight," spoke to his horse and they were off.

"I'm bound for Windmill Point," said Allen. "There's some fine pine timber there that Father wants me to look at," he continued proudly; for although Allen was only seventeen years of age his father declared that the boy could "draw a plan for a schooner, select the timber, build and sail the craft"; so Allen had a right to be proud.

Barbara Anne, seated behind her brother, and clasping him tightly that she might not slip from the broad saddle, for the moment quite forgot all her grievances toward Doris. It was a morning in early May, 1774; the air was fragrant with the scent of the climbing honeysuckles that grew over the walls and ran wild along the banks bordering the highway. A little breeze from the wide spreading waters of the Chesapeake lifted Barbara's curls, and fluttered the skirts of her flounced blue muslin. Birds called from the trees along the highway, and as they turned into the road that ran along the water-front Allen quickly drew his horse to one side, for Governor Eden's big coach, with its mounted outriders in scarlet liveries, was coming along at a rattling pace.

Allen removed his hat and bowed low as it dashed past; but Barbara Anne heard him mutter an angry word.

"Don't you like Governor Eden, Allen?" she asked, as he swung the big horse back into the road.

"Oh, I have naught against him, save that he has no right to be Governor," replied the boy. " 'Tis high time America had its own government! But, of course, a little girl like you, Bab, knows naught of these great matters. All America is aflame to protect our liberties. 'Tis small wonder that I grumble at even so excellent a man as Governor Eden, since he must obey the English King."

"Oh, Allen! I am past eleven, and I did not think you would talk about my not understanding things, just as Doris is always doing," responded Barbara Anne, giving but little thought to Allen's talk of America's liberties. "Eleven is not so very young," she continued plaintively. "I guess girls can do some things."

Allen chuckled delightedly at the thought of his small sister taking any part in the great conflict between England and America that already seemed inevitable unless the British government ceased levying unjust taxes on the American Colonies. Allen Browne had that very morning been urging his brother Oric to give up the position he held with Governor Eden, telling him that no true American should be in the employ of an English governor; but Oric had only laughed at his young brother's suggestion, calling him "only a boy," and asking him what a lad of his age could know about such things. Allen, recalling this, was now ready to sympathize with his small sister, and said pleasantly:

"Well, Bab, eleven is not being a baby, is it? And I'll wager you would have more courage than Doris in the face of danger. Doris is always too careful of her fine clothes to think of much else."

A happy smile crept over Barbara Anne's face at her brother's words. The big horse was traveling at a smooth trot, and as the little girl felt the soft air on her face, and looked off across the blue waters of Chesapeake Bay, that noble arm of the sea which had so much to do with the life of the people of Maryland, she felt herself a very fortunate girl even if she was the youngest of the family.

"Allen, Doris makes up words about me!" she announced, quite sure that her brother would disapprove of "barbarous," a word she had never heard before that morning.

"Does she, indeed! Well, Doris is a clever girl, after all," Allen replied.

"But Allen, she was not clever! I was singing, and Doris called to me to stop making 'barbarous' noises," declared Barbara.

Allen shouted with amusement.

"Bab, Doris did not make up that word. Don't you know what it means? It means cruel, rude, uncivilized!" he explained.

Barbara Anne's smile vanished. Her lips drew together, and she was nearly ready to cry. If "barbarous," a word so nearly like her name, meant all those hateful things, she was sure that her own name had an even more undesirable meaning; and she became so silent that Allen wondered what was the trouble, and turned his head to smile at the sober-faced little girl who clung so tightly to his riding-coat.

" 'Barbarous'! 'Barbara'!" whispered Barbara Anne, a little questioning note in her voice.

"Oh, yes! Well, they do sound alike, don't they?" Allen agreed; "but you know your name means 'rare'; that is, something fine and unusual. And 'Anne' means 'grace.' So you ought to be well pleased with it."

Barbara Anne's face brightened instantly.

" 'Rare'! 'Grace'!" she repeated happily. "I s'posed

it meant Aunt Barbara Anne Crowningshield," she exclaimed. "I am so glad you told me," and Barbara Anne again decided that Allen was the very best brother a little girl could have, and nearly forgave Doris in the wonderful discovery of the real meaning of her name.

From the harbor-road Allen turned his horse into a bridle path that led toward the timber he wished to examine; the path was for a time within sight of the harbor, and Allen drew rein for a moment to watch the flight of a flock of wild fowl that rose from a near-by cove and fluttered seaward.

As Allen and Barbara Anne rode on, the little girl suddenly recalled the fact that she had left home without asking permission, and that she was bare-headed, both of which things were forbidden.

"I think I am old enough to do some things without asking," she announced, much to Allen's surprise; but he promptly replied:

"Well, Bab, age hasn't much to do with it. We all have to obey orders; and mine are to look over those tall pines, and see what sort of masts they will make." With a pleasant laugh, Allen brought his horse to a standstill, swung himself from the saddle, and lifted his little sister to the ground.

"Here, Bab, hold Dart's bridle-rein, will you?" he said, handing her the smooth leather rein. "I won't be gone long."

Barbara Anne was well pleased to be left in charge of Dart. She looked at the big horse admiringly, and even ventured to reach up and pat its smooth neck. Dart moved uneasily, and began to nibble at the shrubs, pulling a little at his bridle-rein, but Barbara Anne kept pace with the horse as he stepped from the path to reach after a tempting branch. She began to be a little hungry herself, and remembered that Rissie had said there was to be strawberry shortcake for the noonday dinner.

At this tempting thought her grasp on the bridle-rein unconsciously relaxed, and a sharp swing of Dart's head pulled it free from her hand. Before Barbara Anne could seize it, the big horse was out of her reach, crashing though the laurel bushes. Barbara Anne ran after him as fast as she could, but the shrubs caught at her muslin dress, swaying branches flicked her face, and she made but slow progress. A little woodland stream made the bay horse remember that he was thirsty, and he stopped to drink, and Barbara Anne drew a long breath of relief as she found herself beside him, and within reach of the trailing bridle-rein. She stooped to seize it but at that very instant Dart lifted his head from the brook, shook it vigorously, and with a snort of satisfaction cleared the stream at a leap and plunged out of sight among the leafy branches of the forest.

The brook was too wide for Barbara Anne to jump; but she did not stop to look for a more narrow part; she waded across, her kid slippers and white stockings thoroughly soaked at the first step. Calling, "Dart! Dart! Whoa! Whoa!" she pressed resolutely ahead after the plunging horse. But the distance between them rapidly increased, and when the little girl came out into a rough wood-road, the horse had vanished. She stood still for a moment looking anxiously along the road. Dart was not to be seen, and she could not hear any sound to tell her the way he had taken.

"Oh, dear! What will I do?" thought the puzzled girl, pushing back her hair from her flushed face, conscious that the spring sunshine had become very hot, and that she was tired and uncomfortable. Dart had apparently vanished; she knew it was no use to call after him, and there was no trace on the rough road to show the direction the horse had taken.

"I'd better call Allen," she decided; and standing in the middle of the rough path, she shouted her brother's name, and then stood listening eagerly for some response. But none came. Barbara Anne did not realize the distance she had traveled from the bridle path where Allen had left her with Dart to go for some way into the deep woods of the forest in an opposite direction to that taken by the wandering horse.

"Now what will I do?" she exclaimed, as there came no answering call, and with a little sigh Barbara Anne seated herself on a moss-covered log by the roadside.

"Allen won't know what has become of me, or where to look for me, and I couldn't find my way back through those thick bushes," she thought. "I guess all I can do is to call his name every few minutes." And this she did, but as time passed and there was no answer, Barbara Anne's calls grew less clear, and at the end of an hour she decided it was no use to call. Her throat felt dry and parched, and she began to saunter along the wood-road hoping to find a spring or brook, and at last the sound of the faint murmur of running water made her turn from the path through a little opening in the underbrush, and she soon reached a clear, rushing brook where she drank thirstily, bathed her hands and face, and nibbled at the young wintergreen leaves that sprang up in thick clusters on the border of the stream.

She called Allen's name again, but now without hope that her brother was within hearing.

"I guess I must find a way home myself," Barbara Anne decided. "This brook is rushing off somewhere; probably it empties into the Severn River, and if I keep along beside it I'll come out somewhere, too." And the little girl started sturdily along on the borders of the stream, climbing over rotting logs, pushing through tangled vines, and at last finding herself facing a broad smooth beach and seeing the waters of Chesapeake Bay stretch out before her.

Barbara Anne, in spite of being tired, hungry and footsore, smiled with satisfaction. The sight of the blue harbor with its white sails, hovering gulls, and the fishing-boats in the distance, gave her new courage. "I can get home now," she decided happily, and ran down the beach and looked eagerly along the shore for the sight of some familiar building. But she could see only beach and wooded shores. Nevertheless she trudged sturdily along in the direction that she believed would bring her to Annapolis.

CHAPTER II

BARBARA MAKES A PROMISE

ALLEN went up the slope to the grove of pines and examined them carefully. He felt no uneasiness about leaving his little sister, as it was a path but little traveled, and he did not intend to be long absent. But there was more timber to examine than he had imagined, and it was over an hour before he came running down to the big oak tree near which he had left Barbara and Dart.

The big bay horse was browsing along the path, for Dart had circled back through the underbrush to the very point from which he had started.

Allen ran after the horse, caught his bridle-rein, and supposing Barbara to be close at hand, called her name a little impatiently: "Bab! Bab! Come on! It's past noon, and we must be off for home."

He became a little vexed at her failure to answer his summons, and swung himself into his saddle and rode a short distance down the path; but no Barbara appeared.

"Confound it! I'll wager she's asleep somewhere, and I'll have to hunt her up. I ought not to have brought her," thought Allen, and now began to look each side of the path, to call his sister's name, and at last he become thoroughly alarmed. He remembered that bears were often seen in these woods, and at the thought that his little sister might have been carried off by some wild animal, the boy could hardly keep back his tears.

But after an hour's frantic search, he realized that the best way was to hasten home for assistance. The astonished Dart was sent over the road at such a pace that he must have wondered at his young master.

The big gates of the driveway were wide open and as Dart's hoofs clattered madly over the cobblestones, and Allen pulled him up at the side entrance, half a dozen colored servants came rushing from house and stable to see who was arriving with so much noise.

Allen's father also came out on the wide porch, and gazed in surprise at his son's frightened expression.

"Father! Father! I've lost Barbara Anne!" Allen called, running up the steps, and beginning his story before he reached his father's side.

Doris and Elinor appeared in the doorway, with Rissie close behind them; and as Allen finished by saying that a search party must start at once to look for the missing girl, Doris exclaimed:

"I don't believe Barbara Anne *is* lost. She's probably just hiding out there in the woods, and thinks it great fun to frighten you."

But no one paid any attention to what she was saying. Mr. Browne with Allen beside him was hurrying toward the stable, and Rissie had run into the house to find Mrs. Browne and tell her the startling news. It did not take long for Allen's saddle to be changed to a fresh horse, for Mr. Browne and two young negroes to saddle and mount horses, and the little party had clattered out of the yard and were off in the direction of Windmill Point before Rissie had finished telling her mistress that Miss Barbara Anne was lost in the forest a few miles from Annapolis. But before the search party reached the place where Allen had left his small sister, Barbara Anne had encountered a new adventure:

Following the beach to where a rough point jutted into the water, Barbara Anne endeavored to scramble over the rocks, and had just reached the top of a slippery ledge when she heard a murmur of voices. The little girl stood quite still clinging to the ledge, and wondering where the voices came from, for no one was in sight. It seemed to Barbara Anne as if some one was talking close beside her. She held her breath and listened fearfully, for one of the voices sounded gruff and threatening:

"The Tories of Annapolis will have their tea just the same. You'll find cargoes of it coming into port, in spite of all America's fine resolves not to put up with unjust taxation by Britain's King."

Young as she was, Barbara Anne understood the meaning of this, for, although her eldest brother was a secretary for the English Governor of Maryland, she had heard many discussions in her father's house as to the right of the English Parliament to tax the American Colonies. The "Tea Act," as the new English law was called, was bitterly resented, and Americans were determined not to pay a tax levied by a body in which they were not represented. The men of Maryland, in particular, were against it, for Maryland's charter guaranteed her exemption from British taxation.

"We'll know how to deal with tea cargoes," Barbara Anne heard another voice declare. "The Boston 'Indians' showed us how to do that last November when they boarded the English ship and emptied the tea chests overboard."

This was followed by chuckles of laughter, and at that moment a tall figure appeared from behind the rocks where Barbara Anne crouched.

"What's this? What's this? Someone spying on us!" he exclaimed, seizing Barbara Anne by her shoulders and lifting her up so that she found herself clear of the ledge and gazing at a number of men who were stretched out on the rocks.

At the sound of their companion's voice, they started up, and seeing only a little bareheaded, ragged girl gazing at them with frightened eyes, they began to laugh loudly.

But the tall man, still holding Barbara Anne by the shoulders, did not laugh. His eyes were fixed sternly upon her as he asked:

"What were you doing hiding behind that ledge? Tell me that, young woman! And who brought you here to spy upon us?"

"If you please, I'm lost!" Barbara Anne responded, in so husky a whisper that the other men could not hear what she had said.

" 'Lost,' " repeated the tall man, lowering her to the ground very gently but not relinquishing his grasp. "What d' you mean by 'lost'? You're miles from any house. Someone must have set you ashore here; now own up; tell me exactly how you came here and what for."

"I came with Allen, and the horse ran away, and I can't find Allen, so I'm lost. Anyway, I s'pose I am," Barbara Anne exclaimed, gaining a little courage as she realized that, in spite of their gruff voices, there was nothing very terrifying about the men. They looked like the planters and farmers who could daily be seen about the streets of Annapolis.

"Allen? Allen who?" demanded the tall man.

"Allen Browne. We live on Francis Street; and Allen went to look at pine trees, for masts, and his horse went off and I went after it; and now I'm lost!" Barbara Anne explained.

"Looks as if we were more scared than hurt, Fletcher," said one of the men with a friendly smile toward Barbara Anne. "The little girl's dress is torn, and I can well believe she has had a long walk, and is tired out and hungry. Is that not so, little maid?"

Barbara Anne nodded. "Yes, sir. I drank at a little brook, but I am thirsty now."

Two of the men scrambled to their feet, while the man who had discovered Barbara Anne now released his grasp, and said kindly: "Sit thee down in the shadow of this rock, child; we'll have food and drink for you in no time." Barbara Anne was quite ready to obey. She had just seated herself when the two men reappeared, one carrying a basket and the other a pail of fresh water which he set down beside Barbara, handing her a tin cup while the other man lifted the cover of the basket.

Barbara Anne drank thirstily, and ventured to smile a little as she saw the contents of the basket. There was part of a roasted duck, some slices of corn bread, several round brown cakes, and a square stone jar.

"It's well past noon, but I'll wager you've had nothing to eat," said the man called Fletcher.

Barbara Anne gazed at him in surprise. " 'Past noon,' " she repeated. "I haven't had anything except some wintergreen leaves since breakfast. And 'twas not ten o'clock when Allen and I left home."

All four of the men now seemed very friendly. They urged her to eat, and when one of them opened the square stone jar and smilingly announced: "Guava jelly," as he used his claspknife to spread it thickly on the corn bread that he passed to Barbara Anne, she was no longer anxious or afraid. She was sure that these kind men would take her safely home, and she made an excellent luncheon.

While Barbara Anne ate, the men went to a little distance and talked among themselves.

Fletcher had recalled the fact that a young Mr. Browne of Francis Street was a secretary for Governor Eden, and that young Browne's father was supposed to be in sympathy with Great Britain; and as the other men realized that the father and brother of the little girl who had so suddenly appeared at their meeting place on this remote shore, were both "Tories," as friends of the English cause were then called, their former suspicions that she might have been sent there to spy upon them returned; for all over the thirteen American Colonies the people were preparing to resist the unfair commands of England; and these four men were loyal Americans who were planning an organization to join with their sister colonies in the support of American liberties. They had sailed from Annapolis a few hours earlier, and Barbara Anne could now see their sloop anchored a short distance from the beach where a small boat was pulled up well out of reach of the tide.

The man called Fletcher now turned toward the little girl, and seating himself beside her began to ask questions.

"So you are Mr. Stephen Browne's daughter, and live in one of those fine houses near the State House?" he said amiably, and Barbara Anne smiled and answered him politely.

"And what does your father think of all this talk that is being made about Liberty? Does he believe that King George of England has a right to starve us by closing our ports, as he has closed the port of Boston, until we submit to the tyranny and oppression?" he continued.

"If you please, sir, I don't know," responded the puzzled little girl; "that is, I don't know about tyranny and oppression, but I'll ask my father," Barbara Anne responded.

Mr. Fletcher gave a little gesture of annoyance, and now spoke more sternly.

"You must be at least ten years old; and a girl of that age is old enough to understand what I mean when I speak of American Liberty, and the

Independence of the Colonies, and you surely have heard these things talked of," he said.

"If you please, I am past eleven, and Rissie says that I am large for my age. I do know about Liberty and Independence. I have heard my father say that Maryland must defend its liberties!" Barbara Anne answered eagerly, rejoicing that she could remember something of the talk she so often heard in her father's house.

"Um-m," muttered Mr. Fletcher, as if greatly puzzled; and when Barbara Anne went on to repeat what Allen had said that morning that "America should have its own government," his face brightened, and he called to his companions, who gravely listened as Fletcher repeated what Barbara Anne had said.

"It may be that Browne is a patriot; but he is hand in glove with Eden; and it seems to me this little maid may have been told exactly what to say if she were questioned," declared the young man who had given Barbara Anne the jelly. "In any event," he continued, "she has heard too much of our plans to be permitted to run back and tell of finding us here discussing how we can best defend Maryland against injustice. She has sharp eyes, and I'll venture to say will recognize each one of us when she again sees us. Eh, little maid?" he questioned, gruffly nodding toward Barbara Anne, who had listened with a sense of some undefined peril, but who now answered eagerly:

"Yes, indeed! I am sure I will remember all of you, and that your name is Fletcher," with a little nod toward the man who had discovered her climbing the ledge. "And yours is Hammond," she added, looking up at the young man who had last spoken.

One of the other men laughed good-naturedly.

"She's but a small maid and far from home. It matters not what her father thinks; we'd best set her aboard the sloop and get her home before nightfall. Don't pester her with questions," he said.

But Fletcher and Hammond quickly silenced him by asking if he would like to be seized and sent to England for trial as a conspirator against the English government, reminding him that Governor Eden would act quickly at the news that Maryland men were determined to assert the cause of American liberty.

"There's but one way I can see," declared Fletcher, who was apparently the leader. "This little maid must make us a solemn promise that, if we will take her safely to her home, never to tell of meeting us or repeat any word or name she has heard here."

"That may do if you frighten her so she won't dare tell," suggested Hammond, but Fletcher shook his head.

"I have no pleasure in securing safety by threatening a small girl," he gravely responded; "and I'll venture to say a little Maryland maid would not stoop to break her pledged word. Miss Barbara Anne Browne, please to stand!"

Barbara instantly obeyed.

"Now listen carefully," he continued, fixing his sharp glance upon her. "You know what is meant by a promise, do you not?"

"Yes, sir! If you promise to do anything you *must* do it," Barbara Anne replied.

"Exactly! And, if you make a promise *not* to do anything it is equally true that you *must not*. You understand that?" Fletcher gravely questioned.

Barbara Anne nodded.

"Very well. Now I will tell you what we will do: We are going back to Annapolis, and we will take you with us and see that you reach home safely, if you will promise on your word of honor as a little maid of Maryland never to tell anyone that you found us in this place, or any word you have heard us say; or, should you ever see any one of us again, you must promise to act as if you had never before laid eyes on us. Do you understand?"

Barbara whispered "Yes," but rather faintly.

"Repeat it over after me," commanded Fletcher, and Barbara Anne obeyed.

"Now you can promise. If you do not we shall know that you were really brought here to spy upon us; and so we shall sail away and leave you here," said Fletcher; and, in spite of his declaration against threatening a small girl, his tone carried a distinct warning; and for the first time during that difficult day Barbara Anne was ready to cry. But she remembered how Allen despised a "cry baby." Barbara Anne's greatest joy was to win Allen's approval; so now she choked back the sobs, and endeavored not to think of what might befall her if these men sailed away and left her alone in this remote place. Besides that, she could see no harm in making them the required promise. She earnestly hoped that she would never see them again, and she managed to say with apparent courage:

"I promise."

"That's very well. But you will repeat after me: 'I, Barbara Anne Browne, hereby give my word of honor and solemnly promise never to speak to anyone of meeting Fletcher, Hammond and two other men. I also promise never to repeat one word spoken by these men, and I promise never to recognize them if I ever again see them.'"

Fletcher spoke very slowly, stopping at the end of every few words for Barbara Anne to repeat what he had said. This she did very carefully.

"Well done," declared the man who had goodnaturedly defended Barbara; "and now we'd best be off. 'Tis already sunset, and will be near dark before we get into port."

"The darker, the better, since we've no wish to be seen," grumbled Hammond, and the men started toward the rowboat. Barbara Anne followed them;

but she felt very tired, and when Fletcher turned and saw the little girl plodding along through the sand, he had a little sense of shame at his sternness, and said kindly:

"I'll just carry you to the boat, little maid. 'Tis not easy walking through this sand," and he lifted her with great gentleness and carried her to the boat.

The big sloop was soon under sail, and Barbara Anne, in a comfortable seat near Fletcher, who steered the craft, with a coat belonging to one of the men carefully wrapped about her, was no longer afraid or unhappy. She was bound for home. Looking toward the shore she soon began to distinguish familiar places, and when Fletcher lifted her to the wharf in Annapolis, and said pleasantly: "I will walk with you to the head of Francis Street," Barbara Anne clasped his hand confidently and said: "Thank you," and they moved off together through the gathering shadows of the May evening.

CHAPTER III

IT was a very tired little girl who went up the steps of Mr. Stephen Browne's fine house just as the big clock in the hall sounded the hour of nine. It seemed to Barbara Anne that she had been away from home for months, and she wondered where Big Peter, the elderly negro servant, who was supposed to open the front door for visitors and always to be near the entrance, had disappeared.

The wax candles in the sconces on each side of the long mirror gave a dim golden light on one side of the long entrance hall, and there were gleams of candle light from the rooms opening into the hall, but the house seemed so quiet that it gave Barbara Anne the feeling of having entered a strange house. As she stood just inside the door wondering if she should call for Big Peter or Rissie, she heard her own name spoken, and listened involuntarily.

"Somebody has stolen Bab. I'm sure of it. You know, Doris, how pretty Bab is, with her dark curls and brown eyes, and her pretty white teeth."

Barbara Anne's eyes opened widely. It was Elinor's voice! Elinor praising her? Elinor, who was always

33

telling her that she "toed-in like an Indian,"—that she mispronounced her words, and "stared like an owl!"

But someone else was speaking; and Barbara Anne tiptoed toward the doorway and peered in, and heard Doris' response:

"Yes, I know. And Bab was always so happy. Just this morning she was singing in the garden, and I called to her from the window," said Doris, her voice faltering a little as if she were near to tears.

"O-ooh!" murmured Barbara Anne; "and she telling me to stop making 'barbarous noises'! And now praising me! I'm glad she's frightened."

"What was that, Elinor?" Doris exclaimed. "I heard something like a whisper."

"I didn't head anything," Elinor said, but her voice sounded a little anxious.

"I do wish we were not here alone," Doris continued. "Do you believe in ghosts, Elinor? Do you suppose if dear, dear Barbara has fallen in the river and drowned that she'd come back? Her ghost, I mean!"

"Oh, Doris! How dreadful! I hope she wouldn't!" Elinor said quickly.

"She ought to hope I would come back, even if I were a ghost," Barbara Anne whispered huskily, adding "her own little sister."

Her whisper seemed to echo through the quiet room, and Barbara Anne could see that both Elinor and Doris were looking about the shadowy parlor as if half-afraid, and instantly Barbara Anne resolved to play a game with her elder sisters. She forgot that her feet were bruised and painful, that she was tired by the adventures of her long day, and puzzled by the promise she had given Fletcher. Here, she thought delightedly, was a fine chance to make Doris repent of calling her song "barbarous," and even Elinor might be sorry for calling her own little sister an "owl," and for not wanting to welcome as harmless a ghost as that of Barbara Anne's.

"I do wish Mother and Rissie would come," continued Doris. "I don't believe there is a servant left on the place."

"Oh, Big Peter is sure to be about," Elinor replied, and at this Barbara Anne, making her voice sound as husky and ghostlike as possible, whispered:

"Gone, gone, gone!"

"Elinor!" wailed Doris, "did you hear that? Right in this room!" and the frightened girl clutched at her elder sister, and buried her face against Elinor's shoulder.

"Nonsense! It was only the door creaking," Elinor courageously declared.

" 'Barbarous noises! Barbarous noises'!" came the whisper again that now even Elinor could not refuse to hear, and Doris whispered:

"It is Bab's ghost! Oh, Elinor! When she sang——" and now there came in a softer note:

"One sang high, and one sang low——"

But before Barbara Anne could continue Elinor was darting across the room and Barbara Anne had no time to escape. Elinor was holding her tightly and shaking her angrily.

"Well, Barbara Anne Browne! You wicked child! After making Allen nearly sick with worry, and all Annapolis out searching for you, here you are trying to frighten Doris into fits!" and Elinor gave her small sister an extra shake, and was surprised to have Barbara Anne crumple up and fall against her sobbing:

"I didn't! I was lost. I'm tired."

"Pore lille lam'! Wot yo' doin', Miss Ellie?" and Rissie hurried in from the hall, closely followed by Barbara Anne's mother and Allen; and Barbara Anne found herself lifted in her brother's arms while her mother's face was pressed close against her own.

"Carry her up-stairs, Allen," said Mrs. Browne, and Allen, holding Barbara very close as if afraid she might vanish, started toward the stairway followed by Mrs. Browne and Rissie.

Big Peter appeared at his usual post in the hall, and raised both arms in amazement at the unexpected sight of Barbara Anne!

"Fer de lawd sakes!" he muttered, and started off instantly to spread the good news that "lille Miss Ba'b'y Anne" was safe and sound at home.

Elinor and Doris stood for a moment gazing at each other as if they could hardly believe the evidence of their own senses. Doris was the first to speak.

"Bab must have heard us praising her, and saying how pretty she was," she said regretfully.

"Yes, I suppose she did. But I'm glad I found her out," Elinor responded. "I wonder where she has been all day?"

"Lost!" Doris replied confidently. "She said she was lost, and Bab never says what isn't true. I guess she just happened to hear us talk about ghosts and thought it a good chance to frighten us. Let's go upstairs, Ellie, and see if she's all right. She fell over so easily when you grabbed her," and there was a worried look on Doris's face. Although she often teased and found fault with Barbara Anne, she was a loyal sister, and quite ready to forgive Barbara's effort to frighten them.

"Perhaps she *was* lost; but she had no business to creep in like that and listen to what we were saying. Barbara Anne is being spoiled! Just because she is the youngest the boys all humor her. Look at Allen, taking her off with him this morning, and nearly crazy when she disappeared. I do hope Mother will send her to Baltimore to visit Aunt Crowningshield," Elinor responded, for she could not easily forget Barbara Anne's mischievous behavior.

Nevertheless, the two girls went to the door of Barbara Anne's chamber to be assured that all was well; and Rissie, gazing at Elinor disapprovingly, told them that "lille Miss Ba'b'ry" was fast asleep.

"All tah'd out, pore chil'. An' yo' a-shakin' of her, Miss El'nor!" she added reprovingly. "I reckon yo' ma'll sen' yo' on a visit to yo' Aunt Crown'sh'ld; I reckon she will," and Rissie, with a solemn shake of her head, softly closed the door of Barbara Anne's room.

"Send *me* to visit Great-Aunt Barbara Anne Crowningshield!" gasped the astonished Elinor, as she and Doris entered their own chamber and began their preparations for bed; "I'd like to know what for?"

For a visit to their father's aunt, Mrs. Crowningshield, who lived in Baltimore, was regarded by the Browne children as an undeserved punishment, and something to be evaded whenever possible; and Elinor was greatly troubled at the possibility that she, instead of Barbara Anne, might be obliged to make such a visit.

"Well, Elinor, you know you did shake Bab!" Doris reminded her.

"Of course I did! And that's just the way things go in this house," Elinor responded angrily. "Barbara Anne can run away and frighten everybody, and creep in and make-believe to be a ghost, and it's all right; *she* doesn't have to visit Great-Aunt, even if she is named for her," and Elinor threw her kid slipper with such force that it hit against the closet door with a resounding slap.

"Well, Ellie, I guess we're both mighty glad Bab is home safe and sound, and that it wasn't her ghost," said Doris, already in bed, and well satisfied that nothing had been said as to any possibility of her becoming a guest of Great-Aunt Crowningshield.

Big Peter and his fellow servants quickly spread the news of Barbara Anne's safe return, and Mr. Browne, Oric and Richard, with all the friends who had so willingly joined in the search for the missing girl, returned to their homes. It was supposed that Barbara Anne had found her way to the road and trudged home. And, although everyone wondered how it happened that none of those who were searching had discovered her, there were many approving words spoken of Barbara Anne's sturdy endurance in keeping on until she reached home.

CHAPTER IV

A PRESENT

WHEN Barbara Anne came down-stairs on the second morning after her adventure at Windmill Point, she found Allen waiting for her at the foot of the stairs.

"All right, Bab?" he asked, smiling at his little sister, and before she could reply he added: "I have a surprise for you. Come out to the stable as soon as you finish breakfast."

"Oh, Allen! May I not come now? I'm not a bit hungry. Truly, truly, I'm not," Barbara Anne declared, and finished the last three steps of the stairs in a spring that brought her near enough to Allen so that she could clasp both hands about his arm.

"Bab! Don't do that again! Suppose you had slipped and fallen headlong!" and Allen's smile vanished. He began to fear that his small sister was too ready to take chances. "Being lost an entire day is a sufficient amount of adventure for you for one week, without adding a broken nose to the list," he said, starting toward the dining-room where the rest of the family were already assembled.

40

Barbara Anne was greeted by a little chorus of welcoming voices; and even Elinor smiled at the sight of her little sister in her usual place beside their father, and for the moment forgot the unpleasant possibility Rissie had suggested of a visit to Great-Aunt Crowningshield.

In spite of declaring that she was not hungry, Barbara Anne did not refuse the bowl of appetizing porridge and cream that was set before her, and enjoyed the crisp bacon and hot biscuit. But she had finished her breakfast before Allen, and began to move about uneasily until Oric exclaimed: "Bab, sit still or leave the table," and Barbara Anne instantly slid from her chair, and making a little curtsey to her mother, as was the rule of the house for the little girls, she ran through the hall to the terrace and along the path leading to the stables.

"What is the surprise, Allen? Is it another ride?" asked Barbara, well pleased that her brother had not lingered.

"Not this morning. But something you may like even better," Allen replied, as he clasped Barbara Anne by the hand, and turned into a path leading beyond the stables.

"Allen!" and Barbara Anne stopped and looked up at her brother with shining eyes. "I *know* what it is! It's a puppy! It is! It is!" and the little girl danced about in evident delight. But when Allen said:

"Better than that, Bab," her face grew sober. For Barbara Anne was quite sure there was nothing she could like better than a puppy. For several months she had been teasing her brothers to secure one for her. "A puppy that will grow into a dog like Oric's," she had pleaded. For to Barbara, Oric's fine Airedale terrier, named Pounce, with his good manners and friendly disposition, seemed the most valuable possession anyone could possibly have; and the little girl now wondered what Allen could mean by saying that his surprise was "better" than a puppy.

But the sound of sharp yelps close at hand made her look up questioningly, and when Allen said: "Two puppies are better than one, are they not?" Barbara Anne drew her hand from her brother's clasp and ran to the small enclosure from where the sound came.

"Two! Two! Just like Pounce, only littler! Oh, Allen! Do you mean to give them both to me?" exclaimed Barbara, as she gazed admiringly at the carefully fenced inclosure where two young Airedales frolicked happily.

"They belong to you, Bab!" Allen assured her. "I had a chance to buy them yesterday of a man named Fletcher."

"'Named Fletcher'!" repeated Barbara, gazing at her brother with a look of such astonishment that Allen wondered a little at it, but explained: "Fletcher is a fine chap—a true American patriot.

He thinks just as I do, that Governor Robert Eden ought to be sent back to England, and that Maryland should choose her own Governor. Don't you like the puppies, Bab?"

Barbara Anne drew a long breath, greatly relieved to hear that Allen thought well of the man who had exacted the promise that she would not mention his name. She again turned toward the scrambling puppies.

"They are splendid!" she declared, "and I don't believe I can thank you enough, Allen."

"Well, Bab, I bought those puppies so they would take care of you," Allen laughingly replied. "You can't very well get lost with two yelping Airedales at your heels. You must train them yourself; I'll help you for a week or two," and Allen now lifted one of the puppies and gave it to Barbara to hold. In a few moments Barbara Anne had made friends with them both, and when Elinor and Doris appeared she was trying to think of names for her new possessions.

"Are those your puppies, Allen?" Elinor asked. "If they are, I hope you won't bring them into the house. They'd chew up everything," and Elinor looked with disapproving eyes as one of the small dogs endeavored to nibble at Barbara Anne's shoe.

But Doris was kneeling in the path trying to make friends with the other puppy, which Barbara Anne had just put down.

"Oh, Allen! Give one to me!" pleaded Doris. "I'd take such good care of him."

"They're mine. Both of them," Barbara Anne announced, "and I'm sure Mother will let me bring them in the house," and Barbara Anne seized the puppy from Doris, and endeavored to reach the one whose efforts to devour one of her slippers was proving unsuccessful.

"Yes; I got them for Bab," said Allen. "I thought it would make up to her for that hard tramp of hers for which I was to blame."

Doris stood up brushing the dust from her dress. Her face was flushed, and it was hard work for her to keep back an exclamation of disappointment over the fact that Allen did not mean to give her one of the puppies. She felt vexed, too, that Barbara Anne should have pulled the puppy from her grasp. But she managed to keep silent.

On the day when they had all been so anxious and frightened about Barbara Anne, Doris had made the firm resolve that if her little sister might only come home she, Doris, would never again be cross toward her. And this promise was still fresh in her mind. Elinor had turned and was walking swiftly toward the house; she had instantly resolved to ask her mother to forbid Barbara Anne bringing the puppies indoors.

Allen had to start off to his work, after cautioning Barbara Anne in regard to the proper food and care of the puppies, and Doris and Barbara were left alone.

"What is a good name? What names are good enough, Dor?" she asked eagerly. "Isn't it splendid that I have two puppies, all my own! Isn't it, Dor?"

Doris still held the wiggling, uneasy little pup, as she stood looking at her sister as if waiting for Barbara Anne to tell her what to do with it. There was a little silence, and then Doris asked:

"What are you going to name them?"

"Oh, Dor! I can't think of any names that are right!" said Barbara Anne a little plaintively, looking up toward Doris.

"Why don't you call this one 'Bar-bar'!" Doris suggested laughingly, and Barbara Anne's face brightened instantly.

"That is splendid! And I'll name this one 'Dor-dor,'" she exclaimed, and the two girls laughed delightedly, and Doris wished more than ever that one of these wonderful puppies belonged to her.

"Well, take Bar-bar, Barbara Anne. I must go back to the house and study. You know you begin lessons again to-morrow!"

Before Barbara could answer Elinor appeared on the terrace.

"You are not to bring those dogs into the house, Barbara Anne," she said sharply. "I told Mother about them and that's what she said!" And without waiting for any response Elinor went into the house.

CHAPTER V

INVITATIONS

RISSIE came hurrying down the terrace.

"Yo' brudder Oric jes' gwine off wid de Gub'ner," she announced. "I kin' er reckon dar's trubble wid de King ob England!"

"What do you mean, Rissie?" asked Doris. "What have Oric and Governor Eden to do with King George?"

Rissie shook her head solemnly.

"I hears Massa Oric a-tellin' yo' pa dat dar was all sort ob tribulations an' trubble clus to hand. Young Massa say de Sons ob Lib'ty are a-stirrin' up trubble agin de King."

"Oh, we don't care about kings; we want Mother to see these puppies that Allen gave me," said Barbara Anne. "Ask Mother if she won't come out on the terrace."

"Yas, Miss Ba'b'y Anne; I'll tell her wot yo' says. But don' yo' be talkin' dat way 'bout kings!" Rissie responded, rolling her eyes and regarding the girls with evident disapproval.

"Hurry, Rissie!" commanded Doris, and Rissie started toward the house.

"What do you suppose is the trouble?" said Doris as they seated themselves on the soft grass near the steps leading to the house and permitted Bar-bar and Dor-dor to play about beside them. "I heard Father say last night that Mr. Charles Carroll was determined that Maryland should resist the invasion of Britain's soldiers."

"What's invasion?" questioned Barbara Anne.

"Oh, Bab! 'Invasion' means going where you are not wanted and making trouble," Doris explained, well pleased that she could tell Barbara Anne the meaning of the word, and before Barbara Anne could speak they saw their mother hurrying toward them, and in a moment both the girls were eagerly telling her of Allen's gift to Barbara Anne.

"Where did he discover them?" she asked.

"He—he bought them of a man," Barbara Anne replied, resolved not even to speak the name of Fletcher.

"They are beauties; and we must tell Big Peter to have one of the young negroes keep a special lookout for them, as Elinor does not want them in the house." At Doris's and Barbara's angry exclamation, "Elinor?" Mrs. Browne regarded them with surprise, and Rissie muttered, "Dat Miss Elinor shu' orter go visitin' Mist'ess Crown'sh'ld. She shu had."

"Oh, Mother! Elinor said you did not want the puppies. I do think Elinor——"

But Barbara Anne stopped quickly, remembering that nothing displeased her mother as much as that one of her little daughters should complain of or criticize their sisters. Mrs. Browne apparently took no notice of Barbara Anne's words. She laughed at the names the girls had given the puppies, and said:

"Oric is off to Baltimore, and had no time to bid you good-bye; but he asked me to give you girls a holiday treat to-morrow, and to let you say what it shall be," and Mrs. Browne looked at her little daughters questioningly.

"I love Oric!" Doris instantly declared, rejoicing that she would have an entire day free from lessons, and need not even practice on the fine harp that stood in the parlor, and on which Mrs. Browne herself daily played.

"Can we do anything we want to, Mother?" Barbara Anne asked eagerly.

"Why, yes. I promised Oric that you might," her smother replied.

"Then let's go for a sailing party. Oh, Mother! That would be the best of all! And may we not ask Vera Scott, and Anna Chamberlin and Amanda and Lesbia Blake, and have a picnic dinner somewhere along shore?"

"Why, I think that will be an excellent plan," Mrs. Browne smilingly agreed. "Rissie, tell Mirabel to plan for a big basket of luncheon for a dozen girls for to-morrow, and you and Martin will go with us."

"Yas'm," Rissie replied. But it was evident she was not well pleased with the prospect of a day on the waters of Chesapeake Bay.

"I will tell Allen to have the sloop ready for us early in the morning. And now, girls, you had better go in and change your dresses and Rissie will go with you to invite your friends. You can ask six." Mrs. Browne started to go indoors.

"But what will we do with Bar-bar and Dor-dor?" asked Barbara Anne.

"I will speak to Big Peter about the puppies. You may be sure, dear, that they will be well looked after," replied Mrs. Browne, "and do you not want to ask little Peggy Stewart to go with us to-morrow? You can tell her mother that we will call for her in the morning."

"Yes, indeed," and Barbara Anne was now all eagerness to be off on the pleasant errand of asking her friends to go on the sailing party. She was well pleased at her mother's suggestion to ask little Peggy Stewart. Peggy was only seven years old, but she was regarded with no little admiration by Barbara Anne because of the fact that a fine square stern brig, owned by Peggy's father, Mr. Anthony Stewart, had been named *Peggy Stewart*. It seemed to Barbara Anne there could be nothing finer than this.

"Let us both wear our yellow muslins, Bab," suggested Doris, and Barbara Anne promptly agreed, and when Rissie came hurrying up-stairs to assist her "young ladies" she found both the girls ready to start. Her good-natured face beamed with an approving smile as she exclaimed:

"Yo' does look complete! Yo' shu'ly does."

The little girls did indeed "look complete." Their dresses of pale yellow India muslin with bands of delicate embroidery, their wide sashes of white silk, and their kid strapped slippers over the finest of white cotton stockings, and their wide flower-trimmed hats, were exactly the proper costumes for two little Maryland maids to wear on a warm May day in the year of 1774. As Rissie hastened to put on the fine crimson silk turban, that Mrs. Browne had recently given her, and a big white apron, and followed her young mistresses down the wide stairway, they were a picture well worth beholding.

"Let us ask Peggy first," suggested Barbara Anne as they walked down the wide street, where flourishing hedges, walls, or high iron fences enclosed the gardens of many a stately home. Before the beginning of the American Revolution Annapolis was known as the most luxurious town in America. Many of the large houses were not only furnished with taste and comfort, but their owners possessed valuable silver services, rare china, and costly furniture brought from France and England. Ships from all seas came into Annapolis harbor. Almost without exception, her settlers belonged to the"gentry" of

England, and Peggy Stewart's father, Mr. Anthony Stewart, was the son of an attorney of King George, an adviser to his Majesty.

The Stewart house, however, faced directly on the street, and as Barbara Anne and Doris, closely followed by the alert Rissie, came near the house, they saw that Peggy and her mother were sitting on the wide porch. Peggy came running down the steps to welcome them, and Barbara Anne nearly forgot her mother's caution to remember to ask Mrs. Stewart's permission for Peggy to attend the picnic before mentioning it to the little girl. She did, however, venture to say: "Peggy! Something splendid is going to happen to-morrow!"

There was only time for this before Doris and Barbara Anne had reached the porch and were making their curtsies to Mrs. Stewart, who welcomed them warmly. When Doris explained their errand, and Barbara Anne, who held little Peggy's hand very closely, added: "And, if you please, Mrs. Stewart, I will keep close to Peggy every minute," Mrs. Stewart smilingly agreed that Peggy might go to the picnic.

"I shall feel quite safe about her, Barbara Anne," she said kindly, and Barbara Anne instantly made the firm resolve that, no matter what might happen, she would not be separated from Peggy either on the sail, or wherever the party might land for the picnic dinner.

CHAPTER VI

PEGGY STEWART DISAPPEARS

THE morning set for the picnic was, as Allen
Browne laughingly declared, "as good as Maryland
can offer, and more than that cannot be said."

The sky was clear, the air soft and warm; and
there was wind enough to promise good sailing. Mrs.
Browne, Barbara Anne and Peggy Stewart were on
board the sloop in good season, before the arrival of
the remainder of the party. The sloop lay at a wharf
on the Severn River, and a footpath led from the
gardens about the Browne mansion across a sloping
field to the water's edge; as soon as Vera Scott
appeared Doris and her friends, with Rissie saun-
tering behind them, started down the path toward
the river.

Allen and Richard were on the wharf and helped
the girls on board the sloop. Allen had just
explained to his mother that neither he nor Richard
could go with the picnickers.

"But I have secured a first-rate man to go with
you and help Ned," he said. "His name is Fletcher,
the man from whom I bought the puppies. He
knows every island and inlet on the Chesapeake.

When Maryland builds a fleet to defend her liberties, Fletcher ought to be made Admiral," and then he explained to his mother that Fletcher had asked if he might bring his own small daughter.

"It seems her mother had planned to go into the country for a day's visit, and Fletcher had agreed to take care of the child. That's why I could secure him," said Allen. "Here they come now," he added quickly, and down the wharf came a tall man carrying a small girl.

"Why, she's a baby!" Mrs. Browne exclaimed.

"No, ma'am! She's nine years old," said the man; and, as he carefully lowered the little girl to the deck of the sloop, Mrs. Browne discovered that the newcomer was not only small and thin but that she was deformed. Her head seemed set directly on her shoulders, and her sharp black eyes peered out in wondering admiration at the group of happy girls in their pretty dresses, and at Mrs. Browne's friendly greeting: "Come and sit by me, little girl, and tell me your name," the little creature only clung more tightly to her father's arm.

"Thank the lady, Amy, and say you'll sit by me," sounded Fletcher's gruff voice; and Barbara Anne, who was perched on the side-rail of the boat just above where Peggy was seated, gave a little cry of terror and lost her balance. But for Ned's swift grasp she would have fallen straight into the water, and as the negro set her down on the deck of the sloop she gazed at Fletcher in amazement.

Doris and Peggy exclaimed laughingly over Barbara Anne, but Rissie gasped in terror as she hastened to smooth Barbara's rumpled frock, and declare that it was a wonder "Miss Bar'b'y wa'n't drownded."

But the others were more interested in waving their good-byes to Allen and Richard, as Fletcher took his seat at the stern and glided the sloop into the channel of the Severn, and turned her bow toward the open waters of Chesapeake Bay.

Close beside Fletcher sat his little daughter, who had not spoken since reaching the sloop. And as Barbara Anne's glance of half-frightened amazement rested upon them she wondered if this could really be the same man who only a few days before had warned her never to speak his name.

Amy Fletcher met Barbara's glance and a little smile crept over her thin face, and at this Barbara moved nearer and said:

"Will you please tell me your name?"

"Amy," replied the little girl.

"Won't you come and sit by me?" asked Barbara; "up near the mast, I mean, where my mother is?" But Amy shook her head, and held more tightly to her father's arm. This friendly, smiling girl was nice to look at, but she wasn't Father, thought Amy. But she liked to have Barbara sit beside her; and when the sloop left the waters of the Severn and entered Chesapeake Bay Amy ventured to ask timidly:

"What is your name?"

"My name is Barbara Anne Browne," responded Barbara eagerly.

"Is your father a Son of Liberty?" questioned the little girl soberly.

The Sons of Liberty was the first patriotic society founded in America for the protection of America's freedom. In 1774 it had been in existence in Maryland for eight years; and in the spring of 1774, when from one end of America to the other the universal cry was "Liberty," the organization was stronger than ever. John Fletcher was one of the humble citizens of Annapolis, but he was chief among those who were determined not to yield to England's invasion.

Before Barbara Anne could reply to Amy's question Fletcher had turned his sharp glance upon her. But, noticing that Barbara had put her arm about Amy, and was smiling at the little girl in a most friendly fashion, a little smile came over his grave face. And when Barbara said: "I don't know, Amy. But if my father thinks it right he's sure to be one," Mr. Fletcher chuckled, and nodded approvingly.

"I reckon you're a patriot yourself, little maid," he said in a half-whisper. "You know to be an American patriot just now is to walk in the plain path of duty."

"Yes, sir," Barbara Anne responded a little faintly, but her fear of Amy's father was growing less; and when Amy began to whisper about a family of wooden dolls that her father had made for her, and to tell of a wooden horse, "about as big as a little dog," and a flock of tiny wooden geese that Fletcher had skilfully carved as toys for his little daughter, she entirely forgot that dreadful moment on the shore of Windmill Point when Fletcher had declared her a spy.

"I wish I could see your wooden dolls, and the wooden horse and the geese," she said eagerly, and it was Fletcher who quickly responded:

"Yes, indeed! You must come and see Amy's dolls. She has a fine playhouse as well," and Fletcher nodded toward Barbara Anne in the most friendly manner, as if he, too, had entirely forgotten their earlier meeting.

Not one of the party had missed little Peggy Stewart, of whom Barbara Anne had promised to take special care. Mrs. Browne, sitting in the bow of the sloop with the girls grouped about her, supposed that Peggy was with Barbara Anne in the stern; and not until Fletcher, following the directions Allen had given him, guided the sloop close in to the wooded shore of a small island, and called to Ned, the young negro boy, to jump ashore and make fast the rope to a stout oak-tree, whose branches overhung the water, did Mrs. Browne realize that Peggy was not beside Barbara Anne.

"Barbara Anne, where is Peggy? Is she taking a nap under the seat?"

"Peggy!" exclaimed Barbara Anne, looking about with startled eyes, and hardly believing it could be possible that Peggy was not to be seen. "Oh, where is she? Where is she?" she called, jumping up from her seat and running toward her mother.

But a sharp word from Fletcher brought her to a standstill.

"Sit down quietly until the boat is made fast. Then we'll find out where the little girl is. I don't recall seeing her," he added thoughtfully.

Barbara Anne obeyed. But she could not keep back her tears. If Peggy was not on board the sloop she must have fallen overboard, thought the unhappy little girl, realizing that if so dreadful a thing had befallen her friend, she, Barbara Anne Browne, was to blame.

The sloop was securely fastened, and one by one the little party went ashore. Then Fletcher searched the tiny cabin, and looked carefully about the deck of the sloop, but without success. There was no sign of the missing girl.

CHAPTER VII

A NEW FRIEND

NONE of the party could now think of anything except little Peggy Stewart.

"She could not have fallen overboard! She couldn't! We would have heard her splash!" declared Barbara Anne tearfully, and Mrs. Browne and Mr. Fletcher agreed that it seemed nearly impossible that such a thing could have happened. But where could she be?

Barbara Anne had completely forgotten Amy in her fears for Peggy, and Mrs. Browne had gravely announced that there was but one thing to do— return to Annapolis—when Barbara felt her hand seized tightly and looked down to find little Amy close beside her.

"Is it a game about the little girl?" Amy asked anxiously. "My father said you would all play games," she added thoughtfully.

"A game about Peggy! Oh, no, no! We are afraid she is drowned!" whimpered Barbara Anne.

"But she's in the box! The box near the mast. I saw her lift the cover and get in," Amy declared.

Without a word Barbara Anne drew her hand from Amy's and darted off to the sloop. No one else had heard what Amy had said, and Elinor and Mrs. Browne both started after Barbara. But the little girl was well in advance of them, and had reached the deck of the sloop calling "Peggy! Peggy!" as she ran toward a square, clumsy box that was securely fastened to the bottom of the boat near the mast, and that usually contained extra ropes, blocks and tackle, and which seemed an unlikely place for a small girl to hide. Just as Barbara Anne was about to lift the cover she stopped short, for the cover of the box was apparently lifting itself and Peggy's curly yellow head appeared; and seeing Barbara Anne she exclaimed, "I've been asleep," and then proceeded to scramble out of the box, her dainty dress crushed and spotted by the coils of rope on which she had rested.

In a moment Peggy found herself surrounded by the entire party, while Barbara Anne kept as close beside her as possible.

Peggy was puzzled by the numerous questions, and looked from one to the other in amazement.

"I just lifted the cover and stepped in; and there were little square holes on each end of the box that I could look out from, and I could see Barbara just as plain!" she explained, utterly unconscious of all the worry and fear her companions had felt over her.

"But what made you think of the box, Bab?" questioned Doris, as they now all returned to the

shore and Ned and Rissie began to open the baskets
and make preparations for the picnic dinner.

"Amy told me! She thought it was a game for
Peggy to hide," Barbara Anne explained, keeping a
tight hold of Peggy's hand and resolved not to be
separated from her until Peggy was safely restored
to her own home.

"Don't know why I didn't open that box,"
Fletcher muttered as he lowered the sloop's big
mainsail, while the others went on shore.

The girls were already eager for lunch, and began
talking over the games they would play afterward.

Amy Fletcher could not run about as the other girls
did. Her father had lifted her from the boat and seated her on a mossy knoll near one of the big oaks, and
after she had told Barbara Anne about Peggy, she
had returned to her mossy seat, and watched the others as they ran happily about or stood in little groups.

"If yo' pleases, Mistress Browne, de lunch am
ready," Rissie announced, smiling broadly as the
girls eagerly declared that they were too hungry to
have waited another moment.

"Wal, I reckons yo's g'vine ter hab a feast. Dar's a
whole ham, wid cloves in it, an' crusted wid sugar
an' baked. An' dar's a basket full ob de bes' biscuit
Ole Marilla could bake; an' dar's chicken, an' cook-
ies, an' jelly—an'——"

"Yes, Rissie," Mrs. Browne interrupted, looking about to make sure that all her young guests were at hand.

Rissie and Ned had spread the big white table-cloth beneath two wide spreading trees and set out the luncheon. As the girls gathered about, seating themselves on the soft grass, and Ned and Rissie began to serve the food, no one for the moment remembered little Amy Fletcher.

Barbara Anne, absorbed in her determination to make up to Peggy for having neglected her during the morning hours, quite forgot the little girl with whom she had so easily made friends.

It was Elinor who, glancing about, caught a glimpse of Amy's bright blue dress under the oak-tree, and whispered to Barbara: "Your little hump-back won't get hungry, will she?"

Barbara Anne, with an exclamation of remorse, instantly scrambled to her feet, drawing Peggy with her, and darted off to where Amy sat.

The little cripple smiled happily as Barbara exclaimed:

"Oh, Amy! I nearly forgot you! Here is Peggy Stewart; she is about your age, and we will help you down to luncheon."

"I reckoned you'd come!" Amy responded. She was well used to being alone, but she had never known unkindness, and was always sure of the friendly intentions of others. "Where is my father?" she questioned, as Barbara and Peggy helped her hobble along and seat herself between them.

"Where is he indeed?" echoed Mrs. Browne, and promptly dispatched Ned in search of Fletcher, who slowly followed the young negro, and seated himself directly behind Amy, evidently well pleased to find that the other girls had accepted her as one of the party. His eyes rested approvingly on Barbara Anne's attention to Amy's needs; the tenderest bit of chicken, the most liberal helping of jelly, and the largest square of cake found their way to Amy's plate. Recalling his first meeting with Barbara Anne, when he had believed the little girl had been sent to spy upon him and his companions, he smiled at what now seemed so absurd an idea.

The girls were now ready for games, and Elinor suggested a dance calling Ned, who always had his flute, to play for them; and in a few moments Amy was smiling with delight as she watched the others dancing happily. Amy had no thought of being "left out"; she was sure there was no one as fortunate as herself: to sail all the morning sitting close beside Father; to make friends with the pretty dark-eyed Barbara; and now to see the girls all dancing while the negro boy played the flute.

"O-ooh," she murmured joyfully, "I guess I'll always remember to-day."

After the dancing Barbara Anne and Peggy came hurrying back to sit beside Amy, and Barbara asked her about the wooden dolls, and the tiny horse of which Amy had told her on the boat.

Peggy listened eagerly. "I wish I had them. Will you give them to me if I will come and see you?" she asked, confident that Amy would instantly agree. For Peggy was accustomed to having every wish gratified. If this queer-looking child had such attractive toys it seemed to Peggy quite right to demand them for herself; and when Amy's face flushed and she shook her head Peggy was instantly angry, and pulling her hand away from Barbara's ran off to join the others.

"Oh, Amy! Peggy didn't know any better than to ask; truly she didn't," Barbara explained hurriedly, for Amy looked as if she were about to cry, as she stammered out:

"P'raps I ought to give them to the little girl! But the dolls are all named, and I love every one of them. And I haven't any others. But p'raps I ought to give them to her. She must want them so much or she wouldn't ask for them," and Amy's black eyes rested pleadingly on Barbara.

"Peggy wants everything she sees or hears about," declared Barbara, "but you are not to give her a single one of your things. Why, Peggy Stewart has everything. She even has a fine brig that sails to England named after her!"

"Tell me some more about what little girls like Peggy Stewart have," pleaded Amy. "You see," she carefully explained, "I don't know any little girls who have dolls and ponies and everything. The girls whom I know don't have anything."

"I make up games to play with my dolls," continued Amy. "I have a game I call 'Indians.'"

And now it was Barbara Anne who listened eagerly while Amy told of the little canoes of birch bark that her father had taught her how to make.

"And I set them on my round table and put my dolls in them, and have them welcome *The Dove*, and *The Ark*, and the first English settlers who came to Maryland," said Amy, resting her elbows on her knees and supporting her elf-like face in her hands.

"What's *The Dove* and *The Ark*?" questioned Barbara Anne.

"Oh, just the vessels that brought the Englishmen in 1633. My father reads me books about them," Amy replied. "And he tells me all about the things he sees when he sails about the islands. Oh, I am just as lucky as Peggy Stewart, am I not, even if there is no fine ship named for me?"

"Amy, may I not come very soon and see your dolls, and play Indian games with you?" asked Barbara.

"There! I get everything I want! I was hoping and hoping that you would sometime come and see me, and now you say you will! Didn't I say I was the luckiest girl in Maryland?" responded the delighted Amy, her face radiant with happiness.

"I wonder what the real reason is," thought the puzzled Barbara Anne. "Maybe I'll find out what makes her so happy when I go to see her toys."

CHAPTER VIII

BARBARA ANNE AND THE BEAR

ALTHOUGH Barbara Anne was eagerly interested in all that Andy said she had not forgotten that she must not lose sight of Peggy Stewart. But seeing that Peggy was walking beside Mrs. Browne Barbara Anne assured herself that no harm could come to the little girl, and was about to continue her talk with Amy when Mr. Fletcher appeared.

"Oh, Father! Barbara Anne is coming to see me!" Amy announced, "and I have told her all about my wonderful dolls. Will you not make a doll for Barbara Anne?" she asked confidently, for Mr. Fletcher had never refused any request of his little daughter's, and she was sure he would promptly agree to this one.

"But Miss Barbara Anne Browne has much finer dolls than any I could make," he said, seating himself beside Amy, and putting his arm tenderly about her misshapen little figure.

"P'raps she'd like a wooden one, too," insisted Amy. But Barbara Anne did not speak; she did not even glance up at Amy's father. For something of the fear she had felt of him at their first meeting at Windmill Point had returned, and she now resolved to leave Amy with her father and run down the beach to join the other girls. With a little smile at Amy, she said:

"I'll run and catch up with Peggy Stewart."

"The daughter of a loyal Tory, of Mr. Anthony Stewart, whose ships bring all the foreign luxuries, tea chief among them, for which we are to pay an unlawful tax. For whoever brings tea into this state is an enemy to the liberties of America. Mr. Anthony Stewart seems not to regard that fact," declared Fletcher, forgetting that he was talking to a little girl.

"But Barbara Anne is not to blame, Father! I am sure she is loyal to America," said Amy.

"How is it, little maid?" questioned Fletcher, realizing that this was his opportunity to discover if Barbara Anne had kept her promise. "Do you believe promises are to be kept?"

"I keep my promises," Barbara replied.

"Then you do more than kings," growled Fletcher, and Barbara Anne hurried after her friends.

"Tell your mother 'tis time we made sail for Annapolis," Fletcher called after her. "'Tis midafternoon, and but little wind. Ask her to please be ready to start as soon as may be."

Barbara promised and was off, running swiftly along the beach toward the ledge beyond which she expected to find her mother, Peggy, and the girls

who made up the party. She climbed the rough
rocks, slipping on the clinging seaweeds that clung
to them, and finally scrambled to the top of the
ledge and made her way down to the rugged shore
that stretched beyond. The smooth beach had
ended on the other side of the ledge, and as far as
Barbara could see there was only the rough shore.

"They must be behind those farther rocks," she
said aloud, and kept sturdily on.

For a moment Barbara stood looking up at this
new obstacle. It was too steep and high for her to
climb, and it ran out into water too deep for her to
wade around it.

"I wonder how Mother and the girls managed,"
she whispered, and then Barbara Anne realized
exactly what had happened: that her mother and
the girls had left the shore for the wooded banks,
and were probably by this time back to the little
clearing and the sloop.

But what Barbara could not know was the fact
that Mrs. Browne had not even climbed the first
ledge, that was at least a mile distant from the high
cliff. She had decided, as the afternoon sun had
grown so warm, to lead the girls up the bank to the
shade of the big trees, where they could rest for a
time, and then make their way back to the boat.
Believing Barbara to be with Amy, and expecting
to find her there on returning to the clearing, Mrs.

Browne felt no anxiety in regard to her little daughter.

"I'll soon catch up with them," thought Barbara Anne hopefully, as she scrambled through the vines and underbrush, and made her way up the bank to where there were open spaces and tall trees, and where, more tired than she had realized, Barbara Anne decided to rest, and sat down close to the trunk of a sturdy hickory.

"P'raps I'd better call; then they'll wait for me," she thought, believing that it was the high cliff that had made her mother turn from the shore, and confident they were not far away. So she called: "Mother! Peggy! Doris!" at the top of her voice, repeating the call a few moments later, and listening eagerly for a response.

"Maybe the wind isn't right," she thought, as she stood up and turned in the direction that she believed bordered the shore, and that would be the way her mother had taken. She was tired, but, remembering what Fletcher had said in regard to its being time to start for home, she hurried on, pushing her way through patches of underbrush, and stopping now and then to repeat her calls: "Mother! Doris! Peggy!"

The deep cool shade of the forest was most pleasant to Barbara. And as the afternoon sun sank toward the western horizon, and the shadows grew deeper she did not realize that the long May day was nearing its end, and that twilight was close at hand. She confidently expected at any moment to hear an answer to her calls, or to overtake those whom she believed to be only a short distance in advance of her. Not until darkness dropped like a veil over the woodland, so that she could not find her way, did Barbara Anne acknowledge to herself that nightfall had overtaken her, and that she could not now hope to find her friends.

For a few moments Barbara Anne stood peering into the gathering darkness. Looking up through the branches of the trees she could see the faint glow of the first stars of evening. From the underbrush came the sounds of little woodland creatures scurrying about for food or seeking shelter for the night. Faint bird-calls echoed through the forest, and the little girl stood there tired out by her long walk, and not knowing what to do.

"They'll be sure to find me. Mother won't go and leave me," she comforted herself, and at that moment a lumbering little creature stumbled over her feet, and growled out its surprise.

"It's a dog! Oh, prob'ly it's lost too!" exclaimed Barbara Anne, instantly reaching down to stroke the rough head that rubbed against her. "Where did you come from?" she questioned, as the creature, evidently well pleased by her friendly greeting, sank down beside her.

Barbara Anne, too tired to stand another moment, sat down close to the newcomer, who with little friendly growls permitted her to lean against its warm body.

"I guess you're a Newfoundland dog. You're so big and your fur is so thick," said Barbara Anne. "I wish you could find my mother for me. Oh, dear! What will I do?" and the little girl now began to cry.

The half-grown cub, for the wandering creature that had stumbled over Barbara was a young bear only a few months old, and who had never before encountered a human being and had no fear of anything that seemed so ready to be friendly as this little girl who snuggled against him and rubbed his rough head in so kindly a way, whimpered in company until Barbara Anne stopped her own sobs to listen to his, and was comforted and amused.

"Well, I'm glad you found me, and I guess you'll take care of me until Mother comes," she thought gratefully, and, tired out, her eyes closed. With her head pillowed on the shoulder of a young bear, in the depths of the forest, Barbara Anne went peacefully to sleep.

A short time after Barbara Anne left Amy and her father, they saw the picnickers coming along the

BARBARA ANNE WENT PEACEFULLY TO SLEEP

beach, and Mr. Fletcher lifted his little daughter in his arms and carried her to the sloop, where Ned was happily engaged in fishing. Rissie had been peacefully napping near the luncheon baskets, which she now picked up and carried toward the sloop.

"Mr. Fletcher is hoisting the sail; that means it is time for us to be off," said Mrs. Browne, as the party drew near the clearing; and the girls all hastened their steps, and hurried on board. Mrs. Browne, supposing Barbara Anne to be with Amy, did not feel a moment's uneasiness about her little daughter, and Ned had unfastened the shore rope, and the sloop was ready to swing clear from the landing place, when Amy's sharp voice called: "Where's Barbara Anne?" quickly echoed by Doris and Rissie; and Mrs. Brown looked questioningly toward Fletcher.

"Miss Barbara Anne started an hour ago along the beach to join you. I thought she was with you," he responded, his sharp glance scanning the shore.

"She must have climbed the ledge in search of us. Rissie, you run along the shore and meet her," said Mrs. Browne; "she may be resting on the other side of the ledge."

"Yas'm," responded the reluctant Rissie, scrambling back to land, and starting off grumbling to herself.

"Hurry, Rissie," called Doris; "we're going to eat the rest of the luncheon—tell Bab she won't get her share if she isn't on hand."

But Amy resolved that Barbara Anne should not miss her share of the chicken sandwiches and guava jelly and the frosted cakes. With a whispered question to Mrs. Browne, who nodded smilingly, Amy carefully selected an abundant supply of the excellent food, wrapped it in a large napkin, and returning it to the covered basket soberly announced: "That's for Barbara Anne."

Rissie was gone so long that Mrs. Browne became uneasy and started after her, while Fletcher watched the descending sun, and became troubled by the delay in starting. The tide had turned, the breeze was lessening, and there was now but little prospect that he could get his passengers back to Annapolis before dark.

But after waiting for the return of Mrs. Browne until sunset, and seeing no trace of any of his missing passengers, Fletcher was about to go in pursuit of them when Mrs. Browne and Rissie were seen hastening toward the sloop.

"Bab isn't with them! What can have happened!" exclaimed Elinor, and she and Doris jumped ashore and ran to meet their mother. In a few moments Fletcher and the remainder of the party, except little Amy, who, from her seat in the stern, peered anxiously after them, were all on shore.

"Barbara Anne is lost, or else she fell from the ledge into the water," faltered Mrs. Browne. "We found her hair-ribbon on the ledge, and we called her name all along the beach. What can we do?" and she turned anxiously toward Fletcher.

"I'll find the little maid," he assured her. "She probably climbed the bank, and may have stopped to rest, just out of hearing. Now, give me that lunch Amy saved for her, for she'll be hungry, I'll warrant, and I'll be off."

Encouraged by Fletcher's words Mrs. Browne and the girls began to hope that Barbara Anne was safe and would soon be with them. And with a few words to Amy, Fletcher was off across the clearing and out of sight.

CHAPTER IX

MR. ALEXANDER STEWART ARRIVES

ALTHOUGH Fletcher had declared it probable that Barbara Anne was safe, he was keenly troubled as to what might have befallen her. As Mrs. Browne had failed to discover any trace beside the hair-ribbon, Fletcher was confident that Barbara Anne must have climbed the bank with the intention of returning to the clearing

"The moon rises early to-night," he thought gratefully, as the deep shadows of the woods closed about him and he stood listening for some call that might give him a hint of the direction Barbara Anne had taken. But the forest was silent save for the movements of birds and squirrels, or of the larger animals of the woods.

A young bear crashed through the underbrush near where Fletcher had stopped for a moment, and brought a new fear for Barbara Anne's safety, for Fletcher knew that many wild animals wandered about on the wooded islands of the Chesapeake.

"There's not much chance of a young bear harming her," he assured himself, as half-grown cubs are, as a rule, friendly unless attacked. But at the thought of the creeping lynx and wildcat he grew more fearful, and hurried on in the direction taken by the young bear, who made no effort to move quietly but crashed through bushes and over rough ground with occasional stops to nibble at some tempting spring bud or berry, or to "woof" warningly at a too bold rabbit or ground-nesting bird. Then the sound of the bear's progress ceased.

"The cub's settled down for the night," thought Fletcher, peering through the shadowy forest. "Hope I won't stumble over him, and maybe his mother," and he stood still, wondering what direction to take, and deciding that it was now time to call Barbara's name; and in a moment his loud calls of "Barbara! Barbara Anne! Barbara Anne Browne!" echoed through the woodland.

The moon, now rising gloriously over the waters of Chesapeake Bay, began to send gleams of light through the forest, and it became possible for Fletcher to choose his way with less danger of stumbling over the roots of big trees, or catching his feet in stout vines. He went slowly, however, repeating his calls, and the cub, against whose warm fur Barbara Anne was so comfortably resting, began to move uneasily as the unfamiliar calls reached his sharp ears and "woofed" his disapproval, wondering what new family of animals had come to his island to live. At last, resolved to go deeper into the forest where he could rest more quietly, and with an easy stretch of his clumsy body, quite disregarding his companion, he was up and away.

As the young bear rose to its feet Barbara Anne's head went suddenly to the ground and she awoke.

"Oh!" she exclaimed, looking sleepily about at the shadowy woods and the long gleams of moonlight that made a path of silver through the woods. For a moment she believed herself in dreamland. The soft fragrant air of the spring night, the faint movement of the young oak-leaves, and the shining path under the trees were exactly like Barbara Anne's vision of fairyland. She held her breath for a second, wondering hopefully if it might not be that a fairy queen, followed by all her train of winged, golden sprites, might not instantly appear in this moonlit wood, and dance their fairy dances.

And then suddenly Barbara Anne remembered what had befallen her: that she was lost in an island forest. She remembered the friendly dog, and looked about anxiously for a sight of him.

"I'd much rather have the dog than even to see one fairy!" she whispered, and then jumped to her feet, for she heard Fletcher's call of: "Barbara! Barbara Anne! Barbara Anne Browne!" sounding so near at hand that she ran forward a few steps expecting to see Amy's father step out into the moonlit path.

"Here I am! Here's Barbara!" she called in response, and Fletcher shouted back:

"Stay right where you are, and keep calling."

Barbara Anne obeyed, and in a short time Fletcher's tall form emerged from the woodland, and Barbara ran eagerly toward him, calling:

"Oh, Amy's father! Amy's father! I'm so glad you came. I was lost!"

"I should say you were! And if I had not followed a young bear I might not have so easily found you," Fletcher responded. "I nearly fell into a brook near here. Suppose we go back and get a drink, and I have a lunch Amy sent you," and he touched his pocket where the well-wrapped food rested.

"I am hungry," said Barbara Anne, "but I'm tired," and she sank down in her former resting place.

"Of course you're tired. But I can carry you as easily as if you were a bird," declared Fletcher. "You see I am used to carrying my own little girl," and he lifted Barbara Anne, and turned back toward the brook.

Barbara was glad indeed for the drink of cool water from the cup of oak-leaves that Fletcher made for her. And as she devoured the sandwich and the cake, resting against the protecting arm of Amy's father, she told him of the friendly dog that had come to her.

"The biggest dog I ever saw," she concluded admiringly. "Do you suppose he was lost, too?"

"No, I reckon just wandering about," Fletcher responded, deciding not to tell the little girl that her forest friend had been a young bear.

"Guess that'll be more interesting to her later on," he thought, with a little shiver at what might so easily have befallen the lost girl.

When Barbara Anne had finished her luncheon Fletcher again lifted her in his arms, and strode off at as good a pace as possible toward the shore. He knew the exact location of the clearing; the moon helped him find his way, and as he went he called from time to time: "All's well! Barbara's coming."

Mrs. Browne and Doris came running to meet them, followed by all the party, but Fletcher cautioned them not to awaken the sleeping girl. He carried her on board the sloop, and settled her gently with her head resting on Elinor's lap.

"It's midnight!" Doris whispered to Peggy, who leaned sleepily against her.

The sloop stood out into the moonlit waters of the wide-spreading Chesapeake, and almost at once Mrs. Browne saw the flare of torches from a boat in mid-channel.

"I believe that boat is out in search of us," she said, and Fletcher agreed with her, and guided the swift-sailing sloop toward the barge, that, manned by a number of strong negro oarsmen, and with Richard and Allen Browne, and Mr. Alexander

Stewart in command, was out searching the harbor for tidings of the missing sloop. Mr. Stewart insisted on taking his little daughter into the barge. Although he listened courteously to Mrs. Browne's explanation as to the cause of their long delay in starting for home, it was evident that he felt Barbara Anne greatly at fault.

Allen swung himself on board the sloop, and took Fletcher's place at the tiller.

"You must be tired out," Allen said with a friendly glance at Fletcher's worn face; and the tall man nodded silently. But he was grateful for the boy's thoughtfulness. He knew Allen was in sympathy with the cause of American freedom, and, in spite of Oric's red coat and service under the English Governor, Fletcher began to hope that the entire Browne family might prove to be American patriots. He felt very kindly toward Barbara Anne, recalling her prompt friendliness toward Amy, and again marveling over the little girl's experience with the young bear.

As the sloop skimmed over the peaceful waters of the Severn and neared the wharf a shout of welcome came from the parents and friends of the picnickers who had gathered there. Mr. Stewart's barge had arrived before them, and the news of the safety of the little party had been the most welcome of tidings. Mr. Browne was the first to step on board the sloop; and after a word with his wife he turned to Fletcher who, with Amy in his arms, was already on the wharf.

"I am in your debt, Mr. Fletcher," he declared handsomely. "My wife tells me of your efforts for my little daughter, and I thank you. You have done me a great service."

Fletcher listened gravely.

"You would do no less for any helpless child, sir," he responded; and, before Mr. Browne could speak, he was gone.

"That's a fine fellow," Mr. Browne declared to Allen admiringly.

"He is indeed, sir. A fine fellow, and an American patriot," replied Allen.

CHAPTER X

SEVERAL weeks passed before Barbara Anne fulfilled her promise to visit little Amy Fletcher, and see the wonderful toys of which she had heard on the day of the eventful picnic. Elinor had gone to Baltimore to visit Great-Aunt Barbara Anne a few days after the picnic, sailing off in one of the fine packets that made weekly trips between Annapolis and Baltimore.

Bar-bar and Dor-dor now ran in and out of the house unreproved; and after the day of the picnic, Allen again insisted that Barbara Anne should always take one of them with her wherever she went.

"That's what I gave them to you for, Bab: to take care of you. You wouldn't have got lost in the woods on the day of the picnic and nearly devoured by a young bear, if you'd had one of the puppies with you," he had said.

"But I didn't even see a bear, Allen!" replied the astonished girl. "And a nice dog came, a great, big dog, and made friends with me. I wish we could find that dog again," she concluded soberly.

"'Dog'! Why, it was a young bear! Fletcher is sure of it. He followed young bruin through the woods almost straight to where he discovered you," said Allen. "I suppose the cub didn't know you would be good to eat, or didn't happen to be hungry," and Allen put his arm about his small sister with a grateful sense of the care that had surrounded her.

Barbara Anne was very quiet for a moment. "A young bear," she repeated gravely. "Maybe bears want to be friends with us and don't know how," she added.

"Maybe they do, Bab!" responded Allen, "but I'll feel safer about you if this smart Dor-dor runs about with you."

"Allen, will you take me to see Amy Fletcher?" asked Barbara, as Allen said he must be off for a walk. "I promised to go weeks ago. She will think I have forgotten her. And she has wonderful toys, Allen! I don't s'pose any little girl has toys as fine as Amy's," Barbara Anne added.

"Tell Mother just where we are going, and that we will be at home in good time for dinner," he said, "and take the puppies along. Fletcher will like to see how they have grown."

"Oh, Allen! That will be splendid!" declared Barbara Anne, and ran down the path to the terrace and into the big entrance hall, where she encountered Doris.

"I'm going to see Amy Fletcher, Dor! Tell Mother Allen is going to take me, and we'll be home early," said Barbara.

"Where are your dolls, Amy?" Barbara Anne had eagerly questioned, as she entered the little cabin and been introduced to Amy's mother. Amy nodded smilingly, and insisted that Barbara Anne should sit down in a small cushioned rocking-chair. The rockers of this chair were carved to resemble a swan, and the arms were like birds' wings in shape, while the back of the chair was surmounted by an eagle carved from wood, and skillfully painted.

Barbara Anne had regarded the chair admiringly.

"It's the prettiest chair I ever saw, Amy!" she declared. "I guess Peggy Stewart would he sure to want this chair if she could see it."

"Does she want everything?" asked Amy, as she smiled happily at Barbara's admiration of one of her dearest possessions.

Barbara Anne nodded, as she rocked back and forth in the wonderful chair. "Oh, yes! Peggy knows she can have anything. Why, her father tells the captain of the brig *Peggy Stewart* to be sure to bring her home the finest toys from London," replied Barbara, "but she has no chair like yours, Amy."

"My father made it. And that is an American eagle on the top. My father says the eagle is the strongest and freest bird in the world, and that it will be the emblem of American liberty," said Amy, who now limped across the room and opened the door of a closet.

"O-ooh!" exclaimed Barbara Anne, jumping up from the chair and running to stand beside Amy in front of the closet, gazing in amazement at what seemed to be an exact copy of her own home. There was the fine mansion with its terraces and gardens, and the tiny summer-house. On the terrace were the little figures of three girls, and on the driveway was a coach and four cleverly-carved wooden horses.

"Amy, why didn't you tell me!" exclaimed the amazed Barbara Anne. And when Amy reached up and opened the front door of the house and Barbara saw a small black figure that she declared looked exactly like Big Peter, Amy laughed with delight.

"My father made it all for me, except the little girls; I made those," she said.

This surprised Barbara Anne more than anything she had seen, and when Amy hobbled to another closet and showed her visitor a small work-bench with its complete set of small tools, planes, saws, knives, tiny chisels, and boxes of little wooden pegs of various sizes, Barbara Anne was as admiring as even Amy could wish.

Then, from this same closet, Amy drew out the wooden horse of which she had told Barbara Anne on the day of the picnic, and the wooden dolls, and the birch bark canoes.

Mrs. Fletcher moved a low round table between the two closets, and drew up beside it the rocking-chair and another small chair and the two little girls had just seated themselves when there was a step on the porch and Allen appeared in the open doorway.

"Oh, Allen! I can't go home now. We've just begun!" exclaimed Barbara Anne.

"But it is near dinner-time, Bab. We ought to be at home," Allen responded.

"May not your little sister have dinner with Amy, Mr. Allen? My little daughter has no playmates, and it will give her a great pleasure to have your sister's company. If Miss Barbara Anne can stay my husband will bring her safely home before nightfall," said Mrs. Fletcher.

"Please let me stay, Allen! I am sure Mother will be willing," pleaded Barbara; and Allen, seeing the wistful look on Amy's face, smilingly consented.

"It is most kind of you to ask her, Mrs. Fletcher, and I am obliged to you," he promptly responded, "and I will come for her in the late afternoon;" and bidding his little sister to look after the puppies Allen started for home.

CHAPTER XI

AMY and Barbara Anne smiled happily at each other across the table on which stood four dolls dressed as Indians, two canoes of birch bark with paddles, and a number of small animals carved from wood.

"I wish I could make a canoe," said Barbara Anne, and Amy instantly offered to teach her, hobbling to the closet and bringing a roll of silvery birch bark that had been peeled from the big trees that Fletcher cut down for fire-wood.

It did not take long for Amy to show Barbara Anne how to bend the narrow strips of pliant ash for the frame of the canoe, and, when that was completed, to carefully fasten the birch bark over it; but before it was finished Mrs. Fletcher called the girls to dinner, and hand in hand Amy and Barbara Anne went toward the kitchen where the table was spread for the midday meal.

There was no shining damask or glittering silver, such as Barbara Anne was accustomed to. A coarse white linen cloth covered the table; the spoons were of pewter, and the knives and forks were steel; the dishes were of earthenware. But in the center of the

88

table a. pewter bowl filled with crimson roses gave a festive air to the simple meal, and Amy exclaimed over it admiringly.

"My mother always does the nicest things!" she declared, as they took their seats, and Mrs. Fletcher helped the girls to the perfectly broiled partridge, the baked sweet potatoes, and filled the brown earthen mugs with creamy milk.

Mrs. Fletcher's thin face brightened at Amy's words.

"I have some fine strawberries for you, and the corn bread will be ready in a jiffy!" she said, nodding happily.

" 'Tis a fine dinner, is it not, Barbara Anne? And am I not indeed a fortunate girl to have everything a girl could ask for?" demanded the happy Amy, and Barbara Anne promptly replied:

"Yes, indeed! I never tasted such good potatoes! And, oh, Amy, may I have the canoe for my own?"

"Of course it is yours. And I have a present for you, Barbara Anne. Something I made for you myself," replied Amy.

The strawberries and hot corn-cake proved as good as the partridge; and when Barbara and Amy called the puppies into the kitchen to give them saucers of milk and bits of crust, Barbara Anne began to believe all that Amy had said about her good fortune, and to wish that she and Doris might live in a cabin where they could learn to make their own toys and eat in a pleasant kitchen near an open door that looked out upon the placid waters of the Severn River.

She was eager to return to the little work table and finish the canoe, and wondered to herself what the present, of which Amy had spoken, could possibly be.

Barbara Anne had been so intent on her own thoughts that she had for a moment forgotten her canoe; and when she felt Amy's hand touch her own she gave a little exclamation of surprise, at which Amy laughed aloud.

"I was thinking about your father, Amy," she explained. "I guess he's an American patriot, isn't he?" she ventured.

"Yes, indeed! Of course he is," declared Amy. "Isn't your father?"

Barbara Anne looked very serious at this question. Amy seemed so sure that it was a very fine thing to be an American patriot that Barbara Anne hoped her father was one, but she was not quite sure.

"Amy, tell me just what an American patriot is. I'm not sure that I really know," she acknowledged.

"Of course you know, Barbara Anne! Why, an American patriot is a man who thinks more about America than he does about himself. I have heard my father say that a patriot would suffer anything to make his land a safe and happy place for a free people."

Barbara Anne listened eagerly, and when Amy had finished she nodded approvingly. "Then my father is a patriot," she declared, "because I know that's just what he would do; and my brothers are patriots too."

Amy shook her head.

"Not the grown-up one—not the one who wears a scarlet coat and rides beside the English Governor; he isn't a patriot," she said.

"Oh, Amy! That's Oric, and I am sure he would do all that you say an American patriot would do!" Barbara Anne said.

"Then he mustn't wear a red coat," Amy soberly rejoined. "But do you not want the present I have for you?" she added, pushing a package across the table toward Barbara Anne, and Barbara instantly forgot all about Oric's scarlet coat in her eagerness to see what Amy had given her, and carefully unwrapped the package, smiling in anticipation of its contents. When she held in her hand the figure of an Indian warrior, its face painted, and wearing a tiny head-dress of real feathers, and holding a bow and arrow in its hands, she exclaimed over it in delight, admiring Amy's skilful work, and saying that it was the finest gift she had ever possessed.

Mrs. Fletcher came in from the kitchen well pleased to hear Barbara's praise of Amy, and to see Amy's delight and happiness.

When Allen came after his little sister Barbara Anne was reluctant to leave, and not until Amy had promised to come very soon for a day's visit at Barbara Anne's home, did she begin her preparations to go, putting on her hat, and putting her canoe and Indian "doll" into a pretty basket of sweet-grass that Mrs. Fletcher insisted on giving her.

"I never had so nice a visit as this," Barbara earnestly declared, as she bade Amy and her mother good-bye. "And I do think you are luckier than even Peggy Stewart, Amy."

"Why, of course I am," responded the little girl, as if surprised that there could even be a question.

"Are you an American patriot, Allen?" Barbara questioned, as they reached the terrace.

"Of course I am!" came the quick response. "There's only one Tory in this family, Bab, and I've hopes of Oric."

"Is it Oric's red coat that's the trouble?" asked Barbara Anne, and Allen again laughed heartily as he replied:

"That's it, Bab! If we could get rid of Oric's scarlet coat he'd be all right. Governor Eden has sailed for a summer in England; and Oric had best change his coat before he returns."

Doris came running to meet them, and Allen did not notice Barbara Anne's exclamation.

"If a scarlet coat was all that prevented Oric from becoming an American patriot," thought Barbara Anne, "why, it would be an easy matter to attend to." And while she told Doris all the delights of her day's visit with Amy Fletcher, describing the chair with its carved eagle, and the wonderful playhouse on the closet shelf, Barbara Anne's thoughts were busy over a plan to capture Oric's scarlet coat; for the little girl began to be very sure that until Oric became an acknowledged patriot she could not feel really safe or happy.

And when at the supper table that night she heard her father say that the inhabitants of Maryland had subscribed liberally for the relief of the city of Boston, and forwarded several vessels loaded with provisions, for the citizens who were suffering under England's endeavor to starve them into submission to unjust laws, Barbara Anne again promptly asked:

"Are you an American patriot, Father?"

"Well, my child, do you suppose I could be a friend of Charles Carroll's, of Matthew Tilghman's and William Paca's and be less than a supporter of America's liberties?" responded Mr. Browne soberly.

"Oric wears a scarlet coat," said Barbara Anne, and instantly a shadow seemed to fall over her father's face, and for a moment no one at the table spoke.

Then Mrs. Browne, with a little sigh, said quietly: "We must hope Oric's scarlet coat will soon disappear."

And at this Barbara Anne's resolve became even more determined. If no one dared to take Oric's scarlet coat away from him, so that he too could become an American patriot, why she, Barbara Anne, would do it. And she would not delay, she decided, for her father was saying that Maryland's patriots were to hold a meeting in Annapolis on the 22nd of June; that would be the coming week. It would never do for Oric to wear a scarlet coat at such a time, she thought.

CHAPTER XII

BARBARA ANNE SUCCEEDS

BARBARA ANNE and Doris shared a large chamber that overlooked the slope of the garden toward the river. The room had been furnished especially for the two girls: there was a closet for Barbara Anne's clothes, and a closet for Doris's clothes; and each of these closets was fitted with deep drawers, with a low shelf to hold their shoes, and with hangers for their dainty muslin and silk dresses.

The room contained two small beds, two chests of drawers, and two washstands. Each washstand held a big flowered china bowl and pitcher. There was a light stand between the two beds, and on it stood a tall brass candlestick; there were two small chests of drawers with a narrow gilt-framed mirror hanging over each one, and there were several comfortably cushioned low chairs. The windows were hung with white muslin curtains, and on the polished floor were several rugs.

A smaller room opened from this large chamber, and this smaller room was Elinor's. Across the upper hall opposite these two rooms was the large chamber used by Richard and Allen, and Oric's room was directly across from Elinor's.

Oric was not always at home, however, as his attendance on Governor Eden had required him to spend a good portion of his time at Governor Eden's fine mansion, which, with its handsome court and garden sloping to the water's edge, was one of the most beautiful of Maryland's estates.

On the night after Barbara's visit to Amy Fletcher, Oric did not appear for the evening meal, and when Barbara Anne and Doris went to their room he had not reached home.

"Let's leave our door open so we can hear Oric when he comes in," suggested Barbara Anne, and Doris gazed at her little sister in amazement.

"Whatever for, Bab?" she questioned. "Do you expect British ships to come sailing into Chesapeake Bay, and want a red coat in the house to prove us loyal to the King?"

"We are not loyal to the King, Doris Carroll Browne," Barbara Anne promptly responded. "Did you not, this very night, hear Father say that he was an American patriot, and that he liked not for Oric to wear a scarlet coat?"

"Well, it was this afternoon I heard him speaking with Mr. William Paca, and they both said they liked not to fight against England, and that they hoped for peace," said Doris; "but you are only a little girl, Barbara Anne. Why do you talk so much about great affairs?"

It had been several weeks since Doris had spoken to Barbara Anne as if she were much younger than herself, and as usual, Barbara quickly resented it.

"I s'pose sometime I'll be as old as you are, and know everything," she said, and then added pleadingly: "You don't care if the door is open, do you, Dor?"

"Oh, no; if you want to be waked up by Oric's clattering up the stairs at midnight, *I* don't care," responded Doris, and as Rissie now came hurrying into the room ready to brush Doris's thick waving hair, and make the two little girls comfortable for the night, no more was said about closing the door.

"W'at yo' reckon Miss El'nor doin' in Balt'more?" questioned Rissie. "I 'spec' she's a-wishin' herse'f home."

"What for, Rissie? Is it not a fine thing to sail up Chesapeake Bay and visit Great-Aunt Crowningshield?" questioned Barbara Anne.

Rissie chuckled as if greatly amused by the question.

"I reckons maybe grown-up folks'd enjoy theirselves a-visiting yo' a'nt—I reckons they would so! Dar's a turrible lot o' bowin' an' a-curtsyin' in Mistress Crown'sh'el's house! Dar shu'ly is! An' folks is 'spected to mind der manners in dat house! Sit up straight in der chairs, an' keep der voices low an' pleasant," and Rissie rolled her eyes and lifted her hands as if to express her wonder at Madame Crowningshield's customs.

"Well, Elinor likes to act grown up. She'll have a good time, even if Mother did plan it to improve her disposition," said Doris.

"Don' yo' be talkin' 'bout yo' sister's dispersation," warned Rissie. "Yo' say yo' prayers an' go ter sleep."

And Barbara Anne, thinking Doris was exactly like Elinor, slipped into bed. Rissie extinguished the candle, and in a few moments there was no sound to be heard in the quiet room.

But Barbara Anne did not at once go to sleep. She was resolved to keep wide awake until Oric was in and safely asleep. She lay watching the white curtains as the breeze swayed them to and fro; the fragrance from the garden drifted in and filled the chamber with the mingled sweetness of blossoming roses and honeysuckle. Now and then she heard the sleepy note of some nesting bird; and at last, in spite of her resolve, Barbara Anne went to sleep.

When, a few hours later, she suddenly awoke, she found the room in darkness. She could not even see the white curtains as she sat up in bed and peered about her, recalling her plan to creep into Oric's room, capture the scarlet coat, and hide it in the closet of Elinor's room.

"I'll have to creep to his room and listen. Oh, I do wish I could have a candle," she thought, dreading to step from the safety of her bed into the darkness that filled the room.

"I guess I can do something to help make Oric an American patriot," she thought. "If nobody else thinks enough about it to take away his scarlet coat I s'pose I must," and she stepped carefully to the floor, and stood listening for some sound from Doris.

But Doris slept peacefully on. A little surprised whimper from the two puppies who slept in a basket just outside the chamber door, made Barbara Anne fearful of discovery; but at her whispered command Bar and Dor became quiet. Barbara Anne, with outstretched hands, made her way through the dark hall to Oric's door. Touching the wide paneling her fingers at last reached the latch and she cautiously lifted it, and the door on its silver hinges swung back silently.

Standing just inside the room Barbara Anne tried to peer through the shadows and discover if Oric was in his bed. Although she could only discern the shadowy outlines of the room she quickly realized that her brother was in bed and asleep. But how could she find the scarlet coat? Perhaps he had hung it carefully in the closet! For a moment Barbara Anne felt herself defeated. If she went stumbling about in search of his coat she was sure to awaken her brother; and what excuse could she give for wandering about in the dead hours of the night?

"Prob'ly Mother would send me straight off to visit Great-Aunt Crowningshield," she thought as she moved cautiously along the wall toward where she knew a chair usually stood.

"Maybe the fine scarlet coat will be on the chair," she thought hopefully, sure that her fingers would be able to discover the coat by its number of buttons, the braided collar and pockets.

Fortunately for the success of her plan Oric's coat rested upon the back of the chair, and as soon as Barbara Anne's fingers discovered its buttons and braid, she gathered it up in her arms, made her way from the room and, without closing the door behind her, tiptoed across to Elinor's room and entered. Very softly she pushed the door until its latch clicked. Then with a long breath Barbara Anne made her way to Elinor's closet, opened the door, and pushed the coat hurriedly toward the back of the lower shelf. "I'll come in and hide it in the morning," she thought, as she turned toward her own chamber, to be welcomed by loud barks and to stumble over one of the puppies who rushed to meet her.

"Oh, dear! Quiet, Bar; down, Dor!" she exclaimed, as Doris started up in bed calling out: "What is it? What is it?" and in an instant, before Barbara Anne could scramble to her feet a light shone through the open door and Rissie, candle in hand, appeared.

"W'at's de trubble? W'at yo' chillun makin' sich a commotion 'bout?" she asked anxiously, as she lifted Barbara Anne to her feet and drew her toward the bed.

"Oh, Rissie! It's Bab's fault. She would leave the door open, and the puppies came in. I s'pose Bab tried to get them out without waking me, and fell over in the dark!" Doris explained in a loud whisper, for Rissie's cautioning: "Ssshh—don' be 'sturbin' ebberybuddy," made her careful not to speak aloud.

Barbara Anne listened gratefully to Doris's explanation. Now, she thought, she would not be questioned.

"Go away, Rissie! And shut the door," she said anxiously.

"Dat all de t'anks I gits fer pertectin' yo'," grumbled Rissie, as she softly closed the door behind her.

"I guess I shan't get to sleep again," sighed Doris complainingly. "You know how the least sound wakes me up, Bab. What are you laughing at?" she added, as Barbara Anne's chuckle of amusement reached her ears.

"Well, Dor! I guess I could go all over this house and not wake you up," Barbara Anne responded.

But Doris hardly comprehended. Already she was half-asleep; and a moment later Barbara Anne's eyes closed. The sisters did not awake until late the following morning, and when Rissie came into the room telling them they would surely be late for breakfast, it was Barbara Anne who asked:

"What is the matter, Rissie? What has happened?" for it was plainly to be seen that Rissie was greatly excited.

Rissie lifted her hands, as she always did when surprised or frightened.

"Yo' ma say fer me not to say a w'ud 'bout it," she responded. "But I reckon yo'll h'ar all 'bout de robbers w'en yo' goes down-stairs! Yas, I reckon yo' will. All 'bout de way dey stole Massa Oric's fine coat! Yo' jes' hurry, chillun; I'se got ter be busy dis day! I shu' has."

"Robbers?" exclaimed Doris. "Oh, hurry, Bab," and followed by Barbara she ran down the stairs, eager to hear what had happened.

Doris and Barbara Anne entered the breakfast-room together, and in reply to Doris's questions, Oric, wearing a suit of gray homespun exactly like Allen's, said that the house had been entered by robbers.

"I found my door open and my coat gone. I believe the puppies frightened them away before the rascals could get anything else," he said.

"It's a wonder Rissie did not see the scamps, for Barbara Anne left the door of her room open, and the puppies ran in there and awoke the girls so Rissie went to attend to them. Did you hear any strange noises, girls?" asked Mrs. Browne; and, noticing Barbara Anne's frightened expression, she added quickly:

"As long as only Oric's red coat is taken, I do not think we need worry."

"Now Oric can be an American patriot, can he not?" Barbara Anne eagerly suggested.

"Why, it does indeed seem an excellent opportunity, Oric," said Mr. Browne with a smiling glance at his eldest son. "And I, for my part, will be well pleased if I never see you wear it again."

"But Father! I have heard you say that Maryland's charter from England has given us protection in the past, and that you hoped we might be at peace with the mother country, from which came our ancestors," said Oric, his look fixed anxiously on his father's grave face.

"That is true, Oric. If our charter was not now disregarded by England's rulers, if our liberties were respected, I would still be loyal to England. But the time is near when Maryland must join with Massachusetts and the other American Colonies for the defence of our liberties," and Mr. Browne's glance seemed to question his son.

Oric said no more, and Allen and Richard kept silent.

Barbara Anne moved impatiently, and at last exclaimed:

"Well, I s'pose Oric's an American patriot now, isn't he?"

Oric looked smilingly across the table at the anxious face of his little sister, and rising to his feet he turned his glance toward his father and said steadily:

"I have made up my mind. Henceforth my service is due to America! I will not need my scarlet coat again!"

There was a little murmur of satisfaction as Mr. Browne clasped his son's hand, declaring he could ask for nothing better. Allen and Richard cheered their brother heartily, so that the colored servants, amazed at so unusual a disturbance in the breakfast-room, crowded about the doorway and chattered among themselves.

Barbara Anne was tempted to tell Oric that she had taken his fine scarlet coat, and that it was now safely hidden in Elinor's closet. But she decided to keep her secret for the present.

CHAPTER XIII

ELINOR RETURNS

THE scarlet coat no longer seemed of much importance to Barbara Anne; and not until Elinor's return in late July from her visit to Great-Aunt Crowningshield was it discovered hidden in her closet.

It was Rissie who drew it out from the back of the shelf where Barbara Anne had concealed it, and with loud exclamations of surprise hurried off to tell her mistress of her discovery.

"Dat t'ief mus' been a-hidin' in Miss El'nor's room; an' de lille dogs scart him off. Dey shu'ly did, Mistress Browne," Rissie declared.

Mrs. Browne was inclined to think that Rissie might be right, and it was decided they would not speak to the girls of the discovery of the coat, so Barbara Anne knew nothing about it, when, on the day after Elinor's return, she searched her sister's closet and could not find it.

"Now I can't tell them about creeping into Oric's room in the dark and taking it, and making him an American patriot," she thought. "I can't ever tell about it unless I find the scarlet coat." And Barbara

Anne began to wonder if she had really hidden it in Elinor's closet.

"It was so dark and I was so frightened p'raps I hid it in my closet," she thought, and ran to her own closet and then to that of Doris, searching frantically. She pulled out the long drawers, throwing their contents on the floor, and dragged out the big round flowered pasteboard boxes in which Doris's hats and her own were kept so that when Elinor came into the room she exclaimed in amazement:

"What are you doing, Barbara Anne?"

"Oh, Elinor! I can't find Oric's scarlet coat!" exclaimed Barbara Anne, peering out from the closet, her face flushed and anxious, and her brown curls in disorder. "I was sure I hid it in your closet, and it isn't there, and I can't find it! O-oh!" And Barbara Anne, suddenly remembering that she had not meant to confide in Elinor, clapped her hand over her mouth in horror at what she had said.

"Tell me about it," said Elinor gently. "I'll help you look for it," and before Barbara Anne recovered from her surprise, Elinor had quietly picked up the scattered garments, replaced the hat boxes and the closets were in their usual order, and Barbara Anne had confided to her the story of her midnight visit to Oric's room.

"And now the coat must really have been stolen," she concluded.

"Well, so much the better," declared Elinor, who had returned from Baltimore an ardent supporter of America's right to resist invasion. "We don't want scarlet coats here, and I think you were splendid, Bab, to take it away. You see it really did help Oric. I wonder someone else had not thought to take it before." Elinor looked at Barbara Anne with such evident approval that the little girl's trouble over the lost coat completely vanished, and she smiled radiantly.

"But perhaps you ought to tell Mother about it," Elinor suggested. "We might tell her together; that is, if you wanted me to go with you," and Elinor's friendly smile quite convinced Barbara Anne that she would like to have Elinor with her when she told her mother the story of the lost coat. Barbara Anne now began to wonder about the change in her sister. For since Elinor's return from Baltimore she had not shown any sign of wishing to appear "grown up." She was friendly and patient with her younger sisters, and eager to be a help to her mother. Not only Barbara Anne but all the household noticed the improvement in Elinor, and Mr. Browne laughingly declared that Aunt Barbara had surely taught Elinor a necessary and much needed lesson.

Barbara wondered to herself what this lesson could be; and, as she followed her tall sister to the terrace, she asked eagerly:

"Elinor, what lesson did you learn of Aunt Crowningshield?"

"'Lesson'?" echoed Elinor. "I learned forty lessons. Aunt Barbara thinks girls ought to know everything from good manners to the laws of traffic."

"What's 'traffic'?" Barbara Anne questioned.

"Oh, it's ships sailing back and forth with cargoes," Elinor replied.

"Like the *Peggy Stewart*," said Barbara Anne thoughtfully. "Allen says Mr. Stewart's brig has already sailed from London and will reach Annapolis before Peggy's birthday in November. I doubt not there'll be a fine present on board for Peggy."

" 'Tis to be hoped there'll not be tea on board the *Peggy Stewart*," said Elinor, for Maryland had been one of the first among American Colonies to resolve not to receive any article from Great Britain on which an unjust tax was demanded; and tea was the chief of these. In spite of Boston's resistance against receiving tea, and the fact that Maryland, as early as 1769, had driven from her ports ships loaded with contraband goods, various Tory merchants were attempting to bring tea into the provinces; and it was natural that Elinor should at once wonder if Mr. Anthony Stewart, who was known to be an ardent Tory, might not endeavor to land whatever goods he pleased.

CHAPTER XIV

ELINOR'S "LESSONS"

ELINOR, Barbara Anne and Doris were all in Elinor's chamber at an unusually early hour that evening. The windows were wide open to the warm summer air, and the girls could hear the murmur of voices from the terrace where Mr. and Mrs. Browne and their sons were sitting.

Elinor had established herself on the broad window-seat, while Barbara Anne and Doris piled up cushions on the floor beside her, where they could look out into the shadowy garden.

"Now tell us about the lessons Great-Aunt Crowningshield taught you," said Barbara Anne eagerly.

"Did she ever punish you?" Doris asked.

"I don't believe she ever really intended to punish me," said Elinor, "and I didn't really have any lessons at all!"

"Oh, Elinor!" exclaimed Doris and Barbara Anne in chorus, and Barbara continued: "Father said you had learned a 'necessary lesson.' You must have had lessons."

Elinor smiled thoughtfully. "I know what Father meant," she responded; "he meant that I had learned to think about other people occasionally. I'll tell you as well as I can about Great-Aunt Crowningshield: First of all, she seemed to think I was really a grown-up young lady!"

"But Elinor! That's what you were always wanting to be!" declared Barbara Anne.

"Yes, indeed! You always said you were grown up!" Doris added, a little accusingly.

"Well, I shan't ever pretend again. It isn't easy to be as grown up as Aunt Crowningshield expects every girl to be. Why, Barbara Anne, I do believe she would think that you, who are only eleven years old, ought to know the history of Maryland from the time *The Dove* and *The Ark* sailed into Chesapeake Bay up to this very minute, and exactly how to behave no matter what happens!" and Elinor looked at her little sisters questioningly as if expecting them to be duly amazed. But neither Doris nor Barbara Anne showed the least surprise.

"Great-Aunt Crowningshield was 'shocked,' that's what she said, 'shocked,' that I could not play on the guitar; and she thought I had not made much progress in playing the harp. 'A young lady of your age,' she was always saying. And she said she wondered what my mother had been thinking of that I had not received any instruction in French and Latin! And she mentioned young ladies of Baltimore, who she said were younger than I, who could speak French as well as they could English.

"And she asked if I could dance! And when I said I was to have lessons the coming winter, she said she feared it was almost too late for me to learn easily, and offered to teach me herself."

Barbara Anne and Doris laughed aloud at the thought of anyone as old as Great-Aunt Crowningshield, who was nearly sixty, teaching anyone to dance, but Elinor shook her head.

"Great-Aunt Crowningshield can dance beautifully!" she declared. "She taught me this," and springing up Elinor ran to the centre of the floor and went through the graceful steps that she had learned from Great-Aunt Crowningshield, greatly to the delight of Doris and Barbara Anne, who instantly tried to imitate her.

"And what else?" persisted Barbara Anne, who began to think that after all it would be good fun to visit an aunt who could teach you to dance.

"Why, that is the way it was all the time. I did not have any regular lessons, but Great-Aunt was always being 'surprised' that a young lady of my age was not either practising on her harp, or 'busy with her needle,' or practising the dancing steps, or trying to write as fine a hand as Great-Aunt herself."

"Can Great-Aunt Crowningshield write beautifully?" questioned Barbara Anne.

"She can indeed! She can do everything beautifully," declared Elinor, "and she expects everybody else to. I did not have a minute for fun! She often said that, of course, 'a young lady of my age,'" and Elinor made a little grimace at the words, "did not care for games."

"Did you not get acquainted with any girls?" asked Doris.

"Only 'young ladies,'" Elinor responded. "Great-Aunt took me to call on a number of really grown-up young ladies; I do believe they thought I was as old as they, and she had a party for me, and it was all as if we were as much as twenty! But you should see Great-Aunt Crowningshield make a curtsy! I'm sure no one ever did it so gracefully. I practised at that, too. 'Tis no easy thing to sink to the very floor and to rise as smoothly as a flower."

"Show us, Elinor!" pleaded Barbara Anne, and Elinor, with a light touch on her full skirts, sank gracefully and rose lightly, like a flower indeed; and Doris and Barbara Anne exclaimed admiringly.

"We'll practise that way," they said.

"I am so glad to be home," Elinor said, smiling happily. "I can act like a real girl now, and have good times with you. It's hard work to be really grown up the way Great-Aunt Crowningshield expects you to be."

"And she is a Tory, isn't she?" questioned Barbara Anne.

"No, indeed! She says there is a fine soldier, George Washington, who fought bravely in the French and Indian Wars, and who ought to be put in command of an American army to defend the Colonies," said Elinor.

At an early hour the next morning Barbara Anne was at the entrance of the driveway leading to her father's house, on the outlook for Amy, and she had not long to wait before she saw Mr. Fletcher's tall form coming down the street carrying Amy in his arms, for the little girl could only walk short distances.

Barbara Anne ran to meet them, and Amy was now eager to be set down that she might clasp Barbara Anne's hand and walk beside her to the house.

Mr. Fletcher smiled kindly down on Barbara Anne. He had heard the story of Oric's scarlet coat, and he was now assured that all Barbara Anne's family were loyal to the cause of American freedom. And now, recalling that May morning at Windmill Point when he had exacted so solemn a promise from Barbara Anne, he decided to speak to her of it, and said:

"Well, Miss Barbara, I was just thinking of our first meeting, and of the promise you made me!"

"I have kept it; truly I have!" Barbara Anne gravely responded, and Mr. Fletcher nodded approvingly.

"I never doubted but that you would keep it. But think of it no more, little maid. The cause of American freedom grows stronger every day; before long we will have an American army to protect us from invasion."

"And will George Washington be commander of the army? My Great-Aunt Crowningshield says he should be," said Barbara Anne, well pleased to have Amy's father release her from her promise and speak to her in so friendly a manner.

"Why, 'tis full likely he may. Colonel Washington is a member of the Virginia Committee to forward our liberties," said Fletcher thoughtfully, forgetting that his only listeners were two little girls.

"You need come no farther. I can walk slowly on with Barbara Anne," said Amy, smiling up happily at her father's grave face.

"And Allen and I will bring Amy home in the early evening," added Barbara; so Mr. Fletcher turned toward home, well pleased to know that his little girl was to have a long, happy day with Barbara Anne.

Elinor was waiting for them and gave Amy a warm welcome. "I have seen the beautiful presents you have given Barbara, and I have made something for you, Amy," she said smilingly.

"Oh, Elinor! You didn't tell me! What is it?" asked Barbara Anne.

"Amy will let you see it," said Elinor, handing Amy a carefully wrapped, flat package. "But let us sit down before you open this," and Elinor led the way to a broad, low seat in the shade of a wide-branching oak-tree, lifted Amy and fixed a number of cushions about her, and sat down beside her. And when Amy carefully unwrapped the flat package and displayed a dress of muslin with beautifully embroidered flounces, it was Barbara who exclaimed delightedly:

"It's lovely! Lovely! Who made it, Elinor?"

"Why, I did, every stitch," said Elinor, "and I do hope it is the right size, Amy. If it isn't I can easily fix it."

Amy touched the muslin dress caressingly, and smiled up at Elinor with such delight that Elinor's face flushed with pleasure.

"Oh, Amy! I have never given you anything! I do wish I might have given you your first real present," said Barbara Anne, looking so grave that Amy promptly declared that Barbara Anne was always making gifts to her.

"Why, Amy Fletcher!" exclaimed the surprised Barbara Anne, "what did I ever give you?"

"You gave me a box of fine sweets the first day I ever came here, and a cake to carry home to my mother. And the second time you came to see me you brought me a basket full of roses; and the other day—" but Barbara Anne's gay laugh interrupted her.

"Those were not presents, Amy. I'd give those to anybody. A real present is something on purpose for you, something that I wouldn't give anybody else. That," and she pointed to the dress, "is a real present."

"Yes, indeed! It's beautiful. My mother will love to see it," said Amy. "I do thank you, Miss Elinor."

"I'll make you another sometime," Elinor smilingly answered, as she liglitly kissed Amy's cheek. Promising to see the younger girls again before dinner, she turned toward the house to help Doris with a difficult lesson in fractions.

"Peggy Stewart is coming," said Barbara. "She sent word last night that she would come over this morning. She is coming in a pony-cart with two fine ponies to draw it. Maybe she will take us for a ride."

"Here come two ponies now!" said Amy, looking toward the driveway.

"Yes! Yes! Those are Peggy's. Are they not fine? And their harness shines as if it had bits of gold on it!" exclaimed Barbara Anne, as she and Amy watched the approach of two perfectly matched gray ponies, whose gold-mounted harness glimmered in the sun.

The ponies were driven by a negro boy in a fine blue coat; and in the wide pony-cart, that had recently arrived from London in one of Mr. Stewart's ships, sat little Peggy Stewart and her negro maid.

"You stay here, Amy, and I'll go down the terrace to meet Peggy," said Barbara Anne.

Amy was well pleased to sit alone for a few moments, and to take another peek at her beautiful dress. Bar-bar and Dor-dor jumped up on the seat beside her as if determined to keep her company. But only for a moment, for as Barbara Anne vanished from sight they leaped from the bench and with loud barks ran madly after her.

CHAPTER XV

PEGGY'S PONIES

THE gray ponies stamped their small feet uneasily, and pulled at their bridles although the negro boy stood close by them with a firm hand on the reins. Peggy was still in the cart when Barbara Anne came running to welcome her, but the maid had stepped to the ground.

"Oh, Peggy, your ponies are beauties, and what a lovely cart," Barbara exclaimed.

Peggy smiled, well pleased that the older girl should admire her possessions. Although she was not yet eight years old and had been indulged in every way, Peggy was, as her elders expressed it, "old for her years." She realized that no other little girl in Annapolis had a pony-cart that had been brought from London, to say nothing of the fact float the blue silk dress she was wearing had come from Paris, as had the dainty slippers and silk stockings.

"Get in, Barbara Anne!" said Peggy. The seats are as easy as the chairs in my mother's parlor. My father says there are tiny springs in the cushions," and Peggy bounced up and down to prove the comfort of the new cart, and Barbara Anne promptly climbed in beside her.

"My initials are on the side of the cart in gold letters, and on the harnesses, too," said Peggy; "and see my whip: it has 'Peggy' in tiny gold letters right around the handle," and the little girl reached forward to draw the fine whip with its ribboned lash from its holder.

Peggy was so eager to display the whip that she gave it a flourish, snapping it in the air over the backs of the high-spirited gray ponies, who instantly leaped forward knocking over the negro boy as they swept round the curve of the driveway, the shouts of Peggy's maid as she ran wildly after them making them go at an even more rapid pace.

Bar-bar and Dor-dor dashed after the cart with yelps of delight, as if quite sure it was a game intended wholly for their amusement; and before Barbara Anne fully realized what had happened the gray ponies had reached the highway and were off at their best speed. The little cart swayed dangerously behind them, and the frightened girls clung to the seats expecting to be instantly thrown into the road.

Peggy had begun to cry, and her shrieks of terror, added to the barking of the dogs, served to add to the fright of the ponies who dashed on faster and faster, turning from the quiet morning street into a cart-road that ran through an unsettled district, and where there was no one about to come to the girls' aid.

The ponies had quickly outdistanced Peggy's maid and the negro boy, who without telling any of the Browne household what had happened had raced after the swaying cart, only to see it disappear far down the street.

Amy heard the sound of voices, but the part of the driveway where the ponies stood was not to be seen from her bench; and when they dashed toward the highway Amy had only a glimpse of them and thought admiringly of their speed and beauty.

"Peggy's taking Barbara Anne for a drive," she thought, settling herself more comfortably among the cushions and thinking happily of the beautiful dress Elinor had given her, and of how pleased her mother would be when she should see it.

Not for a moment did Amy feel hurt or troubled by any thought that Barbara Anne and Peggy had not asked her to go with them. She had happy thoughts to keep her company. She told herself that no other little girl could possibly be more fortunate. The warm air made her sleepy; and from pleasant thoughts of Elinor's kindness Amy drifted into slumber, never imagining the danger that threatened Barbara Anne.

Peggy continued to shriek from time to time, but the puppies no longer barked. They needed all their breath to keep the pace of the gray ponies.

"I must do something to stop them, I must," Barbara Anne thought, as the cart struck against a wayside bush and nearly swept Barbara from her seat.

"If I could only get the reins I could stop them," she told herself; and then clasping Peggy's arm she said:

"Keep still, Peggy Stewart!"

Peggy's shriek died away in a surprised gulp, and she stared at Barbara with such horrified amazement that Barbara Anne for a moment forgot her fears and smiled; but before Peggy could recover sufficiently to again send forth one of her terror-stricken yells Barbara Anne continued:

"Keep still! I'm going to stop the ponies. Every time you scream you make them go faster."

Peggy made no response beyond a smothered sob. It was perhaps the very first time in her life that she had been ordered to do anything. She began, forgetting her terror for a moment, to feel injured and abused. What was the use of fine ponies with gold-mounted harnesses, a cart from London, and a wonderful whip, she thought unhappily, if another girl dared speak to one in that way. She sank down in the bottom of the cart whimpering angrily.

But Barbara Anne was not thinking about Peggy. Very cautiously she made her way along the seat to the front of the swaying cart, and began to call: "Whoa, whoa, whoa," as she endeavored to reach for the trailing reins that swung loose over the backs of the fleeing ponies.

As Peggy's shrieks ceased, and the barks of the pursuing dogs no longer urged the gray ponies on, they became less frightened; and at the sound of Barbara Anne's voice calling the familiar "Whoa! Whoa!" which they had been taught to obey, the ponies gradually lessened their pace. They were beginning to reach the limit of their endurance, and as they slowed down to a walk Barbara Anne drew a long breath of satisfaction, and when the grays came to a standstill, panting with heat and fatigue and hanging their heads, she was out of the cart in a moment, seized the reins, and called to Peggy:

"Jump out, Peggy!"

But Peggy did not move. She began to blame Barbara Anne for all that had happened.

"I don't want to get out, I want to go home. Turn the ponies and drive me home," she whimpered.

"Get out, Peggy," urged Barbara Anne; "if the ponies start again I couldn't get in the cart or stop them."

"It's *my* cart, Barbara Anne Browne. I can stay in it if I want to," Peggy angrily persisted; and Barbara Anne now realized that she must not hope for any help from her companion; that she must depend on herself not only to look after the ponies and keep them quiet, but to discover a way for Peggy and herself to reach home in safety.

At that moment Bar-bar and Dor-dor came into sight, their tongues hanging, and their rough coats covered with dust. They were too tired from their long run to bark their greeting, and promptly crawled under the pony-cart, glad to be at rest and out of the hot sunshine.

Keeping the reins firmly in her clasp Barbara Anne looked about for a place where she could fasten them, and at last discovered a stout sapling near which the ponies had come to a standstill. It did not take long for the little girl to slip the reins about the tree and tie them securely. She was sure the ponies, even had they not been so tired, could not now free themselves. Then she looked at the tired little creatures, who evidently had no wish to move. Their gray coats were wet with sweat, and they continued to pant.

Barbara Anne remembered that Allen always waited at the stables after a ride to see that the negro boy rubbed Dart, gave him fresh water and food, and she looked at the tired ponies and wished she could do something for their comfort.

"I could rub them off with grass," she thought, and pulling a handful of the tall wayside grass she wiped the head and neck of each pony; and, gaining courage, decided it would not be too dangerous to rub their slender legs; so that when Peggy, kneeling on the cushioned seat of the cart, peered over, she saw Barbara Anne rubbing the ponies and talking to them softly.

"Barbara Anne! I want to go home," she whined.

Barbara did not look up at Peggy until she had quite finished doing her best for the ponies' comfort.

Peggy kept repeating over and over: "I want to go home! I want to go home!" while Barbara Anne sturdily pulled the grass, at first to rub the ponies and then to feed them. She even ventured to gently slip the silver bit from their mouths, and the little creatures whinnied gratefully, rubbing their pretty heads against Barbara Anne's shoulder as if to thank her for thinking of their comfort.

"I do wish I could get them a drink," said Barbara Anne, now turning toward Peggy.

"O-ooh! *I'm* thirsty. Thirsty as I can be; I'm hot and tired! It's all your fault, Barbara Anne Browne. 'Twas your hateful dogs that made my ponies run away," wailed Peggy.

"Peggy Stewart! It was you yourself! You made them run, showing off that hateful whip," Barbara Anne instantly replied, wondering to herself why she had ever imagined that she liked Peggy. "She's a regular Tory, just thinks about herself all the time," Barbara Anne decided.

"I don't like you any more, Barbara Anne," Peggy continued in her whining voice; "and when my father's brig *Peggy Stewart* arrives from London I will not give you any of the preserved fruits or the candied nuts that are on board for me."

"My father says 'tis time Annapolis people stopped bringing things from London, and do without luxuries," declared Barbara Anne. "I care nothing about the things you speak of, Peggy," she concluded, trying her best not to remember the delicious flavors of the sweets that Mr. Stewart's ships so often brought into port.

Peggy was now too angry and uncomfortable to do anything but sob, and Barbara Anne began to feel sorry for her, and remembered that Peggy, after all, was a little girl.

"Of course it isn't as if she were past eleven, same as I am," she thought, and she climbed into the cart and said gently, "Let me take off your bonnet, Peggy; 'twill be cooler without it."

Peggy made no objection to this, and Barbara Anne untied the broad ribbons that held the blue silk bonnet, and drew it from Peggy's head. She smoothed back the damp hair; and, drawing her handkerchief from the pocket of her linen dress, Barbara wiped the little girl's flushed, tear-stained face.

"We are all right now, Peggy; truly we are. I am sure we can find our way home," she said.

"I don't want to walk. Why can you not turn the ponies and drive me home?" said Peggy; "and I am *so* thirsty, Barbara," she added.

It took some time for Barbara Anne to convince Peggy that the only way for them to reach home was to walk; and the little girl at last reluctantly consented. Barbara Anne made sure that the ponies were securely fastened; and then, with Peggy clinging to her hand and the tired dogs close at their heels, they started for the long walk home.

"We'll send your boy back for the ponies," Barbara Anne told Peggy, feeling sure the little girl must feel sorry to leave the pretty gray ponies.

"I don't care anything about them," declared Peggy. "I do think you might have made them bring us home, Barbara Anne. I hate to walk on this rough road in the hot sun," and Peggy hung back so strongly that Barbara Anne's good nature began to fail. She suddenly remembered Amy Fletcher, and that Amy would limp cheerfully on beside her without a murmur or complaint.

"You ought to be glad that you have a straight back, and two good feet to walk with, Peggy Stewart! For your father's ships can't bring you things enough to make you happy," she exclaimed, and Peggy only wailed a complaining response, and demanded to stop and rest.

They were just about to make another start when Barbara Anne saw a figure racing down the road toward them.

"Here comes your negro boy, Peggy," she said, and Peggy's face at once brightened.

"Goody! Goody! I'll make him fetch the ponies and drive me home," she exclaimed joyfully; and when the frightened, tired boy reached them Peggy at once demanded that he should lose no time in going after the ponies; and the boy hurried on, and it was not long before the two girls were again seated in the cart and riding toward home.

Peggy leaned comfortably back in her seat, but she did not look toward Barbara Anne or speak to her. She did not seem to realize that she owed her safety to Barbara Anne's presence of mind and carefulness, and when they reached a turn in the road she called to the negro boy:

"Stop here, Louis; Miss Barbara Anne wants to get out and walk home!"

The boy promptly obeyed. He well knew that his young mistress would quickly make trouble for him if he dared disregard her wishes; and Peggy now gave Barbara Anne an ugly little push, saying:

"You made me walk, and now you can walk. I shall tell my mother 'twas all your fault."

Barbara Anne found herself standing in the dusty road, with the hot July sunshine beating down upon her uncovered head. She looked after the cart, and saw Peggy reach for the fine whip and strike at the ponies.

Looking about Barbara Anne gave a little sigh of relief as she recognized familiar landmarks. Close at hand was the church where she went each Sunday with her father and mother. Her own home was not far distant, so she trudged on, Bar-bar and Dor-dor keeping as close beside her as possible, but it seemed a long time to the little girl before she reached the driveway leading to her own home, and slowly made her way toward the house.

CHAPTER XVI

A NEW PLAN

When Amy awoke from her brief nap she found Elinor and Doris smiling down at her.

"Where's Bab?" asked Doris.

"She has gone for a drive with Peggy Stewart, who came with two gray ponies, and a negro boy driving, and a negro girl with her in a pretty cart," Amy responded. "The ponies dashed off at a great speed, with the puppies running after them," Amy happily explained, as if well pleased to have been left alone.

"I do think Barbara Anne ought to be ashamed! To leave you alone this way," declared Doris, "and it is nearly time for luncheon."

Elinor's smile had disappeared, but she did not find fault with Barbara Anne. "Bab knew that we would take good care of Amy," she said, as she sat down on the bench beside the little girl who was so much smaller than other girls of her age, and whose black eyes now looked up questioningly.

"It's some game of Peggy's. I am sure Bab would not leave you all this time if she could help it," said Elinor; and Doris agreed, for both the girls knew that Barbara Anne was always eager to be with Amy; and Doris started off to question the servants.

But neither Big Peter, Rissie nor any of the negroes had happened to see the rush of the gray ponies when they had raced down the driveway; so it was taken for granted that Barbara Anne had gone with Peggy for a drive; and Elinor and Doris now promptly devoted themselves to entertaining Amy.

"What would you like to do?" asked Elinor.

"To hear you make music!" Amy instantly replied. "Music on the tall, big harp!"

And with Amy hobbling beside her, Elinor at once turned toward the house, while Doris ran upstairs to bring down Barbara Anne's dolls, and her own work-box for Amy to see. An hour passed happily in the cool drawing-room, and Big Peter called them to luncheon, and Barbara Anne was still absent.

Mrs. Browne was seriously displeased when Elinor explained that Barbara Anne had gone for a drive with Peggy Stewart and had not returned, and called Rissie, telling her to go to Mr. Anthony Stewart's and bring Barbara home.

"Yas'm!" responded Rissie, resolving to give Miss Bar'b'y Anne a right sma't talkin' to. But she had just left the house when she saw a forlorn little figure, followed by two tired dogs, coming slowly toward her.

"Fo' de lan' sake wot hab befallen de chile," muttered Rissie, running to meet her young mistress and putting her arm about the bedraggled, tired little girl. Barbara's friendly service for the gray ponies had sadly soiled her white dress; her stockings were gray with the dust of the road; her hair untidy, and her flushed face and her hands were grimy with dirt.

"Oh, Rissie! Peggy made me walk and walk," faltered Barbara Anne, leaning heavily against Rissie's friendly arm.

Rissie nearly carried the little girl into the house. "Yo' better step upstairs, Miss Bar'b'y 'Anne, pore chile, an' let me make yo' tidy," she urged, and Barbara Anne silently obeyed. She was so thirsty after her long walk in the heat of the midsummer day that Rissie hastened to bring cool water, and then drew off the soiled dress and stockings, and very soon Barbara Anne was resting comfortably in her own cool bed. While Rissie had been waiting upon her Barbara Anne told the story of the morning's adventure, and Rissie listened with frequent exclamations of wrath against Peggy's thoughtlessness.

"It do 'pear like dat chile am a spoilt chile," she muttered. "If dat Peggy be dis selfish 'fore she be grown up, I reckon she gwine ter see trubble."

Barbara Anne was so tired that she made no objections to staying in bed for an hour's rest.

"I'll jes' step down an' splain ter yo' ma, honey," said Rissie, "an' bimeby yo' kin spring up an' hab a good luncheon an' play wid de pore lille cripple gal!"

"Amy isn't poor; she's lucky," Barbara Anne called after the retreating Rissie who hurried to the dining-room, and, with many exclamations, and much rolling of her eyes, told the story of Barbara Anne's drive behind the gray ponies.

"Miss Bar'b'y Anne were jus' run away wid; an' das de truf. She nebber 'tended to go. An' dat Peggy jes' 'posed on Miss Bar'b'y Anne, an' 'bleeged her to walk home!"

"Mother! May we not go right up and see Bab? And can we not have luncheon in her room? She must be so hungry!" pleaded Doris; and Mrs. Browne willingly agreed; and followed by Big Peter, who offered to carry Amy up the stairs, she led the way to Barbara Anne's chamber.

It did not take the servants long to draw a round table beside Barbara Anne's bed and spread it with an excellent luncheon.

Mrs. Browne and Elinor soon left the little girls to themselves, and Big Peter brought the box of tools and set it on the table, and the bits of wood Allen had brought from the shipyard; and Amy carefully explained the uses of the sharp knives, planes and tiny chisels.

The two friends worked happily together, and when Allen came in he exclaimed in admiring surprise over the result of their work; Amy had carved a tiny duck so perfectly that it well deserved praise.

While Barbara Anne's work was less skilful, she had made a good beginning, and the clumsy wooden bird that she was just finishing proved that with practise she would soon do nearly as well as Amy.

"Where is your box of paints, Bab? You could paint these birds and make them look even more natural!" said Allen; and Barbara Anne, with an exclamation of delight, jumped up and ran to the drawer in her closet where her toys were kept, and brought back the box of watercolor paints that had been brought to her by Oric on his return from a voyage across the sea to Paris the year before.

It was the first box of paints that Amy had ever seen; and she was eager to see Barbara Anne use the small brushes, and when Barbara Anne suggested that Amy should mix the colors, as Allen directed, and paint the wooden duck she had carved, Amy was highly pleased. And Barbara Anne now realized that she could make Amy a "real present" if she gave her the cherished box of paints, and instantly announced:

"Amy! I am going to give you this box of paints! You do like them, don't you? And they will be a real present!" Barbara Anne was so evidently pleased at having discovered something worthy of being a gift to Amy that she seemed even more pleased than Amy herself, who really felt that it was hardly right for her to accept anything so wonderful.

"P'raps I can paint a picture," Amy said thought-fully, recalling the lovely blossoming vines that grew over the door of her cabin home, and the glimpse of the river, and thinking it would indeed be a splendid thing if she could make a picture of it.

When the time came for Amy to return home, and just as Allen was starting toward the stables to have a trustworthy horse harnessed to the light carriage in which he intended to drive the little girl home, Amy, whose seat was near the window, exclaimed:

"Here comes my father!"

"We will go down to the terrace to welcome him," suggested Allen, lifting Amy and starting toward the stairway, while Barbara Anne carrying the box of paints followed close behind them.

Amy now said her good-byes and her father swung the little figure to his shoulder and started for home, Amy smiling happily over her treasured gifts.

It was while Barbara Anne slept that Mrs. Browne spoke of the letter she had that day received from Great-Aunt Crowningshield. "Aunt Crowningshield is very urgent for Barbara Anne to make her a visit. She truly says that she is hardly acquainted with her namesake," and Mrs. Browne looked toward Barbara Anne's father as if awaiting his decision.

"I expect Barbara Anne will think it a fine thing to visit her great-aunt," said Mr. Browne, "but the Colony is in such an unsettled condition that travel is hardly safe. The Chesapeake is infested by out-laws who are attacking craft of all kinds; they capture travelers, cargoes, and destroy all boats of which they cannot make use. I should not want Barbara Anne to journey to Baltimore by way of Chesapeake Bay."

"If she wants to go, may I not take her on Dart?" suggested Allen. "She could ride on a pillion behind me most comfortably."

"Why, that is not a bad idea, Allen. And you can take a message to the Baltimore Committee of Safety," Mr. Browne nodded approvingly. "I think it an excellent plan for Barbara Anne to visit her aunt if she can make the journey in safety; and I believe Allen will have no trouble."

"'Tis a long ride for a little girl, nearly forty miles, and the roads are not oversmooth," Mrs. Browne reminded him.

"We must think it over. But I believe it can be arranged so the journey will be an easy one," Mr. Browne responded.

CHAPTER XVII

THE JOURNEY TO BALTIMORE

WHEN Mrs. Browne told Barbara Anne, on the day following her runaway drive with Peggy Stewart, of the proposed visit to Great-Aunt Crowningshield, the little girl was at once eager to go. To ride with Allen all the way from Annapolis to Baltimore, to spend one night on the way at the house of friends, as Mrs. Browne said would be necessary, seemed a great adventure to Barbara Anne; and she quite forgot her former visits to her great-aunt and all the discipline and dullness of the long days in the quiet house in Baltimore. She even forgot the pleasant plans she had made with Amy for a picnic in the woods near Amy's home, and for further work with the tools her father had given her.

"How soon can we start, Mother? And how long am I to stay in Baltimore?" she questioned.

"Your Aunt Crowningshield writes that she hopes you will make a long visit. I suppose you must stay at least a month," said Mrs. Browne thoughtfully, realizing that a month would indeed be a long time for Barbara Anne to be away from home, and without playmates of her own age.

"Yes, yes, Mother dear; but when will we start? Will it be to-morrow?" urged Barbara Anne.

"No, indeed! You cannot start until next week at the earliest," and Mrs. Browne smiled at her little daughter's eagerness to be off, realizing that Barbara would soon be even more anxious to come home.

The week seemed a very long time to Barbara Anne. Doris and Elinor declared it was too bad that Bab should have to go to Baltimore just because she had been named for Great-Aunt Crowningshield; but Barbara Anne reminded them that she was to go with Allen; that the journey would take two days, and even Doris acknowledged that such a ride would make up for a good deal.

"I will take care of Bar-bar and Dor-dor for you," said Doris; and at the thought of leaving the puppies behind her Barbara Anne's smile vanished.

It was a pleasant morning in August when, at an early hour, Allen and Barbara Anne made ready for their start on the ride to Baltimore. Dart, his bay coat shining like satin, was saddled and waiting; and at a little distance behind him was the strongly-built brown horse, loaded with bags and baskets, on which Martin would ride.

Mr. Browne lifted Barbara Anne to the pillion, a firm comfortable seat attached to the back of Allen's saddle, and the little girl joyfully realized that the long-planned-for journey was about to begin. Doris and Elinor were bidding her good-bye, evidently wondering how Bab could think there would be any pleasure in a visit to Great-Aunt Crowningshield, and Mrs. Browne was cautioning Allen to take every care of his small sister.

Oric and Richard were not there to bid Barbara Anne good-bye; a few days earlier they had left home to join a party of young men on board a schooner for a cruise down Chesapeake Bay, where, it was rumored, a British cruiser had been seen. The young Americans feared that the Chesapeake was to be blockaded, as Massachusetts Bay had been, and the cruise was to discover if some one of England's ships was really lurking near with the intention of threatening the liberties of Maryland.

Allen was disappointed that he could not be one of this adventurous party; but the fact that he was the bearer of important papers from Annapolis's Committee of Safety to a similar group of American patriots in Baltimore, made him feel that his journey with Barbara Anne was of importance, and he was glad to have his small sister for his companion along the forest roads, and through the lonely stretches of country over which their road made its way.

Allen swung himself into the saddle, and with a word to Dart they were off, with Martin close behind them. Not until they had left Annapolis behind them did Barbara Anne remember that in the excitement of departure she had not even had a glimpse of the puppies. "Doris will take care of them," she thought, and began to fear that before her return the little creatures would have entirely forgotten her. But the morning air was cool and pleasant before the heat of the day began; their road led under the shade of wide-spreading oaks and towering chestnut trees. Squirrels ran chattering about the branches of the trees; the calls of birds could be heard, and now and then flocks of cardinals or blue jays flitted before them. There was the summer fragrance of woods and wild flowers, and Barbara Anne looked about in delight, and thought to herself that nothing could be more pleasant than to ride on in this delightful fashion.

They forded several wide streams, where the horses drank thirstily. At the second of these streams Allen waited for Martin to catch up with them, and lifted Barbara from the saddle that she might not get overtired.

Barbara Anne looked down the road over which they had just come, and in a moment the brown horse came trotting sturdily in sight. Barbara watched it, and gave a sudden exclamation:

"Allen! Allen! Look! What is that running along the road? It's a little animal! Oh! It's one of the puppies!"

Dor-dor, at the sight of Barbara Anne, barked joyfully, and came on with clumsy leaps and bounds.
Splashing into the shallow stream he dashed up the
bank and Barbara found it difficult to keep him
from jumping against her.

Bar-bar had been shut up in the distant kennel,
and Dor-dor, in a comfortable basket, had not
objected to ride until Annapolis was well behind the
travelers. Martin explained all this to his young mistress, with many nods and smiles.

Allen laughed heartily as he imagined what their
aunt would say at the sight of Dor-dor.

"Well, Bab, if she doesn't want him Martin can
take him back," he said, and Barbara Anne began to
feel less troubled.

At noon they made a long rest in a pleasant wayside grove, and once or twice during the afternoon
Allen stopped near some brook or spring, lifted
Barbara Anne from the saddle, and with Dor-dor
beside her the little girl ran about or rested in the
shade. Late in the afternoon they came in sight of
the Lambert mansion, the home of valued friends of
Mr. Browne, where they were to spend the night,
and where they received a warm welcome. There
were no children in the Lambert home, and Mrs.
Lambert declared she would like nothing better
than to have Allen and Barbara Anne stay for the
remainder of the summer.

But when Allen announced that he was carrying important papers to Baltimore, for the Committee of Safety, Mr. Lambert's face became grave.

"There are redcoats on the watch for just such messengers as you, Allen. The Tories are eager for news of what American patriots mean to do in regard to the taxes imposed by England's parliament. If the Baltimore Tories could get hold of papers such as you carry they would think themselves lucky," he said.

"I'd not give them up," Allen declared valiantly.

"How could you help yourself, my lad, if half a dozen stout fellows set upon you?" said Mr. Lambert, and Allen acknowledged that, if so attacked, he could not protect his papers.

Barbara Anne, sitting beside Mrs. Lambert, with the tired Dor-dor resting on the floor at their feet, had been listening earnestly. She had so often heard her father and brothers talk of the determination of the American Colonies not to be enslaved by far-off Britain, she had heard Mr. Fletcher declare that Maryland men would defend their freedom at any cost, that the little girl fully understood that, as a bearer of messages from one American patriot to another, Allen might easily be in danger. And she also had another thought, and spoke quickly:

"If you please, Mr. Lambert, could I not carry the papers?" and her brown eyes gazed earnestly toward the friendly man who had been cautioning Allen in regard to any strangers he might encounter on their journey on the following day.

At Barbara Anne's question he turned smilingly toward her. He meant to make a pleasant answer to the little maid; but suddenly it occurred to him that his young visitor had suggested an excellent plan.

"It is the best thing possible!" he said earnestly, turning toward Allen. "Give your sister your papers. I'll wager she has a deep pocket for them, and if you are accosted to-morrow on the highway, and searched, as may easily happen, they'll not find anything worth their while."

Allen, too, thought well of Barbara Anne's suggestion, and looked toward his little sister with an approving glance.

"You see, Bab, you are to help the cause of America's liberties, if you are only a little maid," he said.

Later on Mrs. Lambert made a deep pocket and stitched it securely to Barbara Anne's flounced petticoat, and Allen's papers were put in this pocket. Barbara Anne went happily to bed that night. Dor-dor was permitted to sleep on the rug inside her chamber-door, while Allen's room was just across the hall. A friendly negro maid had helped her make ready for bed, and promised to call her at an early hour the next morning, and Mrs. Lambert had come in to bid her good-night. But it was not any or all of these safe and pleasant things that made Barbara Anne smile happily to herself as she lay alone in the big bed in the shadowy chamber; she was repeating Allen's words to herself:"You are to help the cause of America's liberties if you are only a little maid," he had said; and, although Barbara Anne found happiness in this, she did not realize that before the end of the coming day she would prove Allen's words to be true.

CHAPTER XVIII

THE MESSAGE IN DANGER

THE sun was just above the eastern horizon when the young travelers bade their kind friends good-bye and started on the last day of their journey to Baltimore.

As Mrs. Lambert bade Barbara Anne good-bye she spoke approvingly of the wide leghorn hat that so well shaded the little girl's face from the sun. It had a high crown, and was trimmed with white ribbons, and Barbara Anne was well pleased that her new friend should praise it. She was about to tell Mrs. Lambert of what was so safely concealed in the top of her hat, when Allen tightened his bridle-reins and they were off.

This morning Dor-dor was not riding in the basket, but trotted soberly along beside Martin. Barbara Anne now and then called to him and the puppy would bark joyfully in response, but Allen at last suggested it would be better for his little sister not to call to Dor-dor.

"You see, Bab, if there are other travelers on the road your calls and the barking of the puppy would attract their attention, and they might wait for us; and it will be as well for us to travel by ourselves.

There's a bridle-path leading 'cross country near here and we will try that," he said; for Allen had often journeyed over this road and was familiar with all the paths, and in a short time he turned Dart into a narrow way where the branches of the closely growing trees brushed against them as the bay horse trotted quietly along over the leaf-strewn way.

"No one could pass us on this path," said Barbara Anne, peering ahead, and then clutching Allen, she whispered: "Allen! Here comes a redcoat!"

Before Allen had time to answer a big black horse loomed up close at hand; and its rider, a burly man in the uniform of King George, quickly drew rein, and he and Allen stared at each other in amazement. Allen was the first to speak; and politely saluting the elder man, said:

"A narrow path, sir! I will back my horse into this underbrush and give you room to pass."

"Thank you, young sir! You travel in some state on so narrow a road. I take it you have come some distance," and the stranger's sharp glance passed over Barbara Anne to Martin, who had dismounted and lifted Dor-dor to the basket.

"From Annapolis," Allen responded, and with a word to Martin, began to back the well-trained Dart to one side of the path.

But the stranger had swung himself from the saddle and seemed in no hurry to go on his way.

"And who is this little maid? 'Tis a long ride for a girl," he continued, with a smiling glance at Barbara Anne.

"My sister, sir!" Allen said briefly. "I am taking her to Baltimore for a visit."

"Well, why not dismount and rest here? I'd well like news from Annapolis. Mayhap you can tell me when the *Peggy Stewart* will make port," said the stranger.

"Not before early October, 'tis said," Allen responded, thinking it wiser to comply with the stranger's suggestion, and dismounting and lifting Barbara Anne from the pillion.

"And how goes the cause of American liberties in Annapolis? Do the rebels Carroll and Paca still talk of treason and rebellion against England's king?" he questioned.

"The freemen of Annapolis talk much of their liberties," Allen staunchly replied.

"And why not? Does not England's Constitution defend the liberty of every loyal man? I fear you are a rebel, young sir," and there was a threatening note in the man's voice as he added: "Do you forget your duty to your King?"

"Your King forgets his duty to America, sir, when he sends soldiers and ships to threaten our liberties," Allen promptly responded; and Barbara Anne no longer felt afraid of this stout English soldier. She was sure that anyone as brave as Allen could face an army.

At Allen's words the stranger gave two sharp whistles, at the same time grasping Allen by the shoulder.

"Very likely you are one of the rebel messengers, for all of your story of taking this little maid to Baltimore," he said, and before Allen could make any effort to free himself there was the sound of jingling harness, and two men mounted on fine horses dashed into sight, and, at a word from the officer, were out of their saddles ready to carry out his orders.

"Come h'ar, Miss Ba'b'y Anne," Martin whispered fearfully, but determined to do his best to protect his young mistress; but Barbara Anne shook her head. She was standing close beside Allen, resolved not to be separated from him.

It was evident that Allen was not at all frightened. War had not as yet been declared between England and her American Colonies; and the English officers in America were, as a rule, cautious of making enemies.

"What have you to say for yourself, young sir?" demanded the stranger. "Are you carrying messages to Baltimore's Committee of Safety? If so hand them over, and save us the trouble of searching you."

"Search if you like," said Allen, "but 'twill be of small use to you."

"If you please, sir, we are going to visit my Great-Aunt Crowningshield," ventured Barbara Anne, and at this the officer's glance became a little less confident. After all, the young rebel was only a boy, he decided, and very likely knew nothing of important affairs. But it would do no harm to make sure, so Allen was thoroughly searched, and the frightened

Martin bidden to unpack baskets and hampers until the officer was convinced that no hidden messages had escaped him.

"And now, little maid, do you know aught of letters or messages? Maybe you are the bearer; 'twould indeed be a clever thought to give them to you to carry," he said, turning to Barbara Anne; and Allen could hardly believe his own ears when Barbara Anne drew her hand from his and said:

"Yes, sir; I have a letter. But I was told not to speak of it until I reached Baltimore. And, if you please, I must not give it to anyone excepting to——" but with a satisfied laugh the officer interrupted her, saying:

"Well, I have made a find! Now let us see this letter. I suppose it is in your pocket?" and he stepped toward Barbara Anne with outstretched hand.

"Oh, no, sir! 'Tis in the crown of my hat!" said Barbara Anne, "and I like not to give it to you," and she looked up pleadingly; and now all three of the strangers laughed heartily, well assured that they had indeed succeeded in securing an important message.

"'Tis a pity, little maid, but I must trouble you for the letter. 'Twas a clever thought to hide it in your hat," said the captain, smiling at Barbara Anne's sober face as she removed her hat and from under its lining drew out a sealed letter and handed it to the stranger.

"Will you please to read it and let me have it again, or my Great-Aunt Barbara Anne will not

"YOU MUST PARDON ME, LITTLE MAID," HE SAID

know that I am to be given a shilling each week to spend as I please," said Barbara Anne, and Allen could hardly restrain his chuckle of relief.

The stranger read the inscription thoughtfully. He was now a little uncertain, and liked not to open a letter addressed to another person; but he reminded himself that it was doubtless a message of traitors against England's laws, and broke the seal. But in a moment he realized that he was mistaken; the letter was about clothing and care of this small maid who stood gazing anxiously at him as if fearing that he might destroy the precious letter.

He carefully refolded it, and taking off his hat bowed low as he gave it back into Barbara Anne's hands.

"You must pardon me, little maid; and you, young sir," he said, turning to the smiling Allen. "These are troublesome times, and it is my duty to prevent treason to the King; and your own words proved you a rebel. But I see you are but children, bound as you truly said on a visit, so go your way in safety."

The two men who had held Allen now released him, and, at their leader's command, led their horses down the path.

Barbara Anne carefully returned her mother's letter to the crown of her hat, and looking up to find the stranger's glance upon her said gravely: " 'Tis a good place to hide a letter, is it not?"

"It is indeed," the man replied, "and I am sorry to have caused you the delay. I could wish so brave a lad were loyal to His Majesty, King George," he added, with a little bow toward Allen.

Allen bowed in response, and lifting Barbara Anne to the pillion, mounted Dart, and followed by the trembling Martin, rode on without a word to the defeated stranger who was now in the saddle and riding after his men.

For a few moments neither Allen nor Barbara Anne spoke, but when they were well out of hearing of the English soldier Allen drew rein, and turning in his saddle exclaimed:

"Bab! You gave me a tremendous fright when you said you had a letter. But when you spoke of the shilling Great-Aunt Crowningshield is to give you each week, it was all I could do not to laugh aloud! You did indeed play a fine joke on King George's officer!" and Allen now laughed so heartily that Martin gazed in amazement at his young master.

"I was afraid if I did not tell him of Mother's letter he might ask what was in my pocket," Barbara Anne soberly responded.

"Ha! ha! ha!" laughed Allen, delighted over the defeat of the stranger. "It will indeed be a fine story to tell when I hand the papers to Mr. Samuel Purriance, and tell him that it was a little maid not yet twelve years old who defeated an English officer and saved the letters. I doubt not the story may even travel as far as Philadelphia."

Barbara Anne smiled happily. "Will our father be pleased?" she questioned.

"He will be proud, Barbara Anne! And when I tell Fletcher of how cleverly you managed he will think you deserve praise from all loyal Americans!" declared Allen. "But we must not linger, for the Tory soldier detained us over long," and chuckling over the defeat of the English officer Allen started Dart on at a good pace.

Allen was now in the best of spirits, and Barbara Anne smiled as she recalled the officer's amazement in discovering that the letter was of no account. When Allen began singing:

> "Hark! hark! the lark at heaven's gate sings,
>   And Phœbus 'gins to rise
>   His steeds to water at those springs
>   On chalic'd flowers that lies;
>   And winking Mary-buds begin
>   To ope their golden eyes,"

she joined in the song, that echoed through the quiet of the leafy woodlands and made Martin nod and chuckle with satisfaction, well pleased that his young master and mistress had so happily escaped any trouble with the English soldiers.

At noontime they rested near a slow-moving stream in the shade of a huge hickory tree. Martin unsaddled the horses, and Allen suggested that Barbara Anne should take off her shoes and stockings and wade in the shallow stream. "That's what I mean to do," he added, and in a few moments they were wading out in the cool water, while Martin opened the basket of luncheon that Mrs. Lambert had given them.

Allen was in the best of spirits as they rode from the path into the highway, where they soon began to meet farmers on horseback or negroes driving mules, and to pass occasional farmhouses. They rested once more by the roadside before reaching Baltimore; and the long August twilight had well begun when the tired horses came to the end of their journey, and Barbara Anne found herself mounting the marble steps toward Great-Aunt Crowning-shield's front door.

Allen lifted the heavy brass knocker, and in a moment the big door swung open and a smiling negro servant welcomed them, saying:

"I reckon Mistress Crown'shield be a expectin' ob yo'. Please to step in," and Allen and Barbara Anne, closely followed by a tired and panting Dor-dor, entered the narrow hall. At the sight of the dog the smile disappeared from the negro's face and he lifted both hands as if too surprised to speak; but a moment later whispered:

"Fo' de land sake! A dawg in dis house! I shu do wonder wot will happen to dat dawg," and shaking his head solemnly he led the way down the hall and opened the door leading into a pleasant room that overlooked a garden in the rear of the house.

The room was dim and shadowy in the twilight, and for a moment neither Barbara Anne nor Allen could see anyone, but Dor-dor instantly rushed toward the end of the room announcing his presence with loud barks; and a tall figure sprang up from a well-cushioned davenport exclaiming:

"Merciful heavens!" and with outstretched arms, as if warding off a dangerous foe, Great-Aunt Crowningshield stood before them.

"Don't be afraid, Aunt Crowningshield, it's only a puppy," Allen said as he sprang forward and seized Dor-dor by his collar and held him firmly.

" 'Only a puppy'? Whose puppy? Who brought him here?" gasped Mrs. Crowningshield, sinking back on the couch.

"He's my puppy, Aunt Crowningshield; but I did not mean to bring him, truly I did not," said Barbara Anne, taking a step forward, and fortunately remembering to make a curtsy as she faced the tall figure of her great-aunt; and a moment later she felt her aunt's arms about her and heard her say:

"Welcome, dear Barbara Anne; and this is Allen, is it not? Allen, who can draw the plans for ships, and then build and navigate them, if I am told aright;" and she released Barbara Anne to clasp Allen's hand and welcome him, and even ventured to touch Dordor's rough head in greeting.

For Mistress Crowningshield had quickly remembered that these young people were her invited guests; and, since they had ventured to bring a dog, the dog must be properly received. Great-Aunt Barbara Anne might seem exacting in demanding that her young nieces should, as Rissie would say, "mind their manners," but she was equally exacting with herself, and now seemed to quite forget Dordor, who had at once settled himself comfortably at her feet, evidently well pleased by his reception.

As Barbara Anne and Allen seated themselves beside their aunt and carefully answered her questions about their journey, a servant came into the room and lighted the tall wax candles in the silver wall-sconces, and Barbara Anne could now see her great-aunt more clearly. The little girl's first thought was that she had never seen such white hair or such shining black eyes; and although Barbara Anne was used to seeing the fine apparel of the ladies of Annapolis, she realized that none of them could wear a more beautiful dress than the silvery gray tissue with its flounces of delicate lace in which Mistress Crowningshield was gowned.

CHAPTER XIX

THE VISIT BEGINS

AT the supper table that night Allen told the story of their encounter with the English soldiers, to the evident satisfaction of Mistress Crowningshield, who nodded approvingly, and declared that, "A quick wit is better than a sharp sword," and smiled so warmly upon Barbara Anne that the little girl decided her great-aunt to be worthy of the beautiful dress she so becomingly wore.

" 'Twill be a fine tale that a little Maryland maid outwitted a clever officer of King George; and it is well the Tories should discover that Americans can think as well as act," said Mistress Crowningshield, and resolved that the story of Barbara Anne's saving the important messages from being discovered should soon reach the ears of various Tory ladies of Baltimore.

Barbara Anne was quite ready to go to bed directly after supper; and, tired out by her long ride, did not awaken until late the following morning. When she entered the dining-room she found that Allen had already breakfasted and had taken the papers from the pocket of her flounced petticoat and gone to deliver them to Mr. Samuel Purriance.

"I bade him not to fail to tell the story of his little sister's quick wit," said Great-Aunt Crowningshield, as she served Barbara Anne's portion of porridge, and smiled at her little niece across the shining mahogany table.

For a moment Barbara Anne made no response, for she was staring at Dor-dor, who after running to meet her, had raced back to sit as near as possible to Mistress Crowningshield, and watched her expectantly as if sure of some bit of food from her hand.

"Why, Dor-dor acts as if he were your dog, Great-Aunt Crowningshield," she exclaimed; and her aunt smiled down at the rough head of the eager-eyed puppy, and replied:

"Why, I suppose he does; he is the first dog that ever entered this house."

"He is a good dog, Aunt Crowningshield. Why, even Rissie, who does not like any dog, says she reckons Dor-dor can't help being a dog," Barbara Anne earnestly responded, eager to defend Dor-dor, but feeling, nevertheless, a little hurt at his desertion.

"I believe I am going to like Dor-dor," Mistress Crowningshield said thoughtfully; "but how came you to give him so silly a name?"

"'Silly'?" echoed the surprised Barbara Anne; and then recalling the day when she and Doris had named the puppies she laughed lightly and said, "I guess Doris and I did not think the names were silly;" and she told the story of the day when Allen had given her the two puppies. Then, in response to her aunt's questions, she related her adventure at Windmill Point, and spoke of Mr. Fletcher and Amy.

Mrs. Crowningshield listened with evident interest; and then Barbara described how cleverly Amy could use tools, told of the little crippled girl's unfailing good nature and her readiness to be pleased, and concluded by saying that she liked Amy better than any other girl in Annapolis.

"And Elinor likes Amy; she has made a beautiful dress for her," she added.

"I suppose you have made something for the little girl?" suggested Aunt Crowningshield. "Not a dress, of course; but you could easily make her some pretty aprons while you are here."

Barbara Anne thought to herself that now the lessons were about to begin, as indeed they were; and when Allen returned from his errand he found his small sister sitting beside a window that overlooked the garden and setting careful stitches in the white muslin apron that her aunt had cut out for her to make for Amy.

Barbara Anne's face was so sober that Allen's smile vanished.

"What's the trouble, Bab?" he asked.

"Nothing; only I don't like to sew!" Barbara Anne responded with a little sigh, "and Great-Aunt Crowningshield says that an hour each morning is none too long a time for me to give to sewing. Then she thinks it will be well for me to have lessons on the guitar, and she means herself to teach me dancing steps, as she did Elinor! Oh, Allen, I don't like visits!" and there was such a pleading look in Barbara's brown eyes that Allen wished he might promise his little sister that she should start home with him on the following morning. But he quickly remembered that little girls must be taught useful things, and resolved not to interfere with Barbara Anne's lessons.

"Where's Dor-dor?" he asked, looking about for some trace of the puppy.

"Oh! Dor-dor is having lessons too," sighed Barbara Anne. "Dick has taken him to the stable, and is to teach him not to bark. Oh, dear," and Barbara Anne's lips trembled and a big tear rolled down her cheek.

"Bab! Mr. Samuel Purriance says that he means to tell the Baltimore Committee of Correspondence of the clever way in which you protected their letter. He even spoke of mentioning it in his next letter to Mr. Samuel Adams, the Boston patriot, that Mr. Adams and his friends may realize how truly all

Maryland is determined to defend its liberties when a little maid is on the alert to protect important letters," said Allen, nodding smilingly at his little sister, whose face instantly brightened.

"Mr. Purriance means to thank you himself, Bab," Allen continued, "and it may be that Aunt Crowningshield will not expect you to sew every day. Come out with me now and we'll see how Dor-dor is getting on."

Barbara Anne glanced up at the tall clock that stood in the corner of the room, and then shook her head.

"I mustn't. It's fifteen minutes more to sew," and she again turned to her work.

"Oh, well! Fifteen minutes is not long," Allen declared. "I'll read to you, that is if there's anything on this bookshelf to read," and he glanced toward the row of books on the top of a secretary.

Barbara Anne looked up hopefully, and a little smile crept over her sober face. If Allen meant to stay with her and read to her she thought the fifteen minutes would go quickly.

"Here's a book about Maryland written a hundred years ago," said Allen, drawing a thin volume from the shelf.

"It says 'A Character of Maryland,' by George Alsop, and it was written in 1662. Let's see what he has to say about Maryland," and Allen turned the yellow leaves and with a little smile read:

" ' 'Tis said the Gods lower down the chain above
That tyes both Prince and subject up in love;
And if this fiction of the Gods be true
Few, Maryland, in this can boast but you.
Live ever blest; and let those clouds that do
Eclipse most States, be always light to you;
And, dwelling so, you may forever be
The only emblem of Tranquillity.'

Time's up, Bab!" declared Allen laughingly, returning the book to the shelf, and Barbara Anne put
away her work and ran after Allen who had opened
a door leading into the garden.

"We'll go and get Dor-dor," he said, and Barbara
Anne, skipping along by his side, quite forgot the
tiresome lessons, and that Allen was to start the
next morning on his ride to Annapolis, and began to
think a visit in Baltimore might, after all, have some
pleasures.

Dor-dor welcomed them with loud barks; but he
was safely shut up and could not run to meet them.

"Oh, Allen! Dor-dor will hate staying shut up,"
exclaimed Barbara Anne, as she ran toward the door
of the small enclosure where Dor-dor was madly
leaping about. In a moment Barbara Anne had
slipped the bolt, swung open the door, and the
delighted Dor-dor rushed out.

"I don't want Dor-dor shut up; and I am going to
tell Aunt Crowningshield so," exclaimed Barbara

Anne, as, with the happy puppy bounding about them, she and Allen turned back to the garden.

"I believe that's a good idea, Bab!" said Allen, "and what's more, I believe Aunt Crowningshield wouldn't want you to be shut up either!"

"Of course I wouldn't!" came the unexpected response, for neither Barbara Anne nor Allen had noticed that their aunt was cutting flowers not far away, and could hear their conversation.

"I intend that Barbara Anne shall play in the garden, or take a walk with Milly, each day," continued Mrs. Crowningshield, "and if she wants the puppy with her at those times, I shall be quite willing."

"Thank you, Aunt Crowningshield," said Barbara Anne, and Mrs. Crowningshield nodded smilingly, sure that she meant to do everything that was possible for the happiness of her little visitor.

"And, as Allen must leave us to-morrow, Barbara dear, you need not undertake any more lessons until he has gone."

"Goody! Goody!" exclaimed Barbara Anne, jumping about the path until Dor-dor, who, believing it a new game for his amusement, barked so loudly that Mrs. Crowningshield declared it would disturb the neighbors, and that Dick had better take the puppy back to the stable.

"Please, please let him stay, Aunt Crowningshield," pleaded Barbara Anne, and her aunt promptly consented. In fact, it was not long before Barbara Anne realized that her aunt never refused any request that her little niece made.

The remainder of the day passed pleasantly; Mrs. Crowningshield had their midday meal served in the garden; and after this she bade Milly bring her the square metal box from an upper closet.

"There is something in the box I want Allen to have," she explained smilingly, and both Allen and Barbara Anne were eager to see what it might be.

Milly placed the box on the table in front of her mistress and Mrs. Crowningshield lifted the cover and took out a worn leather case.

"If we defend our liberties Maryland will need ships and sailors; and sailors will need a compass and sextant, and I think you may be a sailor, Allen; so I want to give you these," and she handed the case to Allen, and added: "Your grandfather for whom you are named used these when he steered his ship into Chesapeake Bay and settled in Maryland."

Allen thanked his aunt gravely. He was greatly pleased to possess these instruments, and promised to take every care of them; and explained to Barbara Anne the method by which the sextant could determine latitude and longitude at sea; and how the needle of the compass, pointing always due north, enabled a navigator to shape his course.

Before Allen had time to carry his new possessions indoors, Dick came hurrying to the garden to announce the arrival of visitors.

"'Tis Mr. Samuel Purriance, an' Mr. William Buchanan, Mistress Crown'sh'ld, an' if you please, dey says dey reques' de pleasure ob seein' Miss Ba'b'y Anne Browne," and Dick made a bow toward the little girl.

For a moment Mrs. Crowningshield and Allen looked at each other in amazement; and then Allen said:

"It is, perhaps, about the meeting with the English soldiers!"

"It is indeed; I am sure of it," replied Mrs. Crowningshield, turning smilingly toward Barbara Anne, and saying:

"Come, my dear, it is evident that you have well served the cause of America's freedom when Baltimore's first citizens do you the honor of a visit."

But Barbara Anne had run to Allen and was clasping his hand, and looking rather troubled and frightened. "If you please, Aunt Crowningshield, I would rather stay with Allen," she said.

"But Allen also must see the visitors; and I expect my namesake to do me credit," said Aunt Barbara Anne. "These gentlemen come to do you honor, my dear; and do not hang back and act like a silly child; remember that you are a young lady."

"'A young lady,'" Barbara Anne whispered the words to herself, thinking it was really rather a dreadful thing to grow up; but she said no more and followed her aunt up the garden path toward the house.

As they entered the drawing-room two gentlemen rose from their seats, and Mrs. Crowningshield greeted them with great cordiality.

"This is my niece and namesake, Miss Barbara Anne Browne," she said with a smile toward Barbara Anne, and the little girl made so graceful a curtsy that her aunt nodded approvingly; and Barbara Anne glancing up at her visitors, two of Maryland's most ardent patriots, thought that not even Governor Eden himself could be more handsomely dressed, for in the years before the Revolutionary War Maryland was one of the wealthiest of the American Colonies. Their ships visited all countries and brought back luxuries of every kind, and the wealthy citizens of Annapolis and Baltimore not only lived in fine mansions but dressed with elegance; and Mr. Purriance and Mr. Buchanan, in their curled wigs, long velvet waistcoats, and braided blue coats, their knee-breeches with silver buckles, their fine stockings and polished shoes, and holding their three-cornered hats, were indeed worthy of Barbara Anne's admiring approval as they bowed in response to her aunt's introduction. Mr. Purriance promptly declared that the object of their visit was to thank Barbara Anne; and he did this in so gracious and friendly a manner that the little girl quickly forgot her shyness; and, seated beside her visitor, she told him of Mr. Fletcher and Amy, of Peggy Stewart's ponies, and of Dor-dor, and her visitor listened with interest.

"I suppose Peggy is the daughter of Mr. Anthony Stewart?" he said, and Barbara Anne eagerly responded that this was so, and that there was a fine brig named after Peggy.

"The brig *Peggy Stewart* will reach Annapolis in early autumn and bring Peggy many fine toys and sweets, as well as dresses," said Barbara Anne, "but I do not like Peggy," she added.

But at the mention of the brig Mr. Purriance had grown thoughtful, and a moment later mentioned to Mr. Buchanan what Barbara Anne had told him in regard to the *Peggy Stewart*.

"Mr. Stewart does not deny that his sympathies are with England; that he wishes the Colonies to submit to injustice. If his brig brings a shipment of tea, as it is full likely to do, what course will the citizens of Annapolis take?" he asked, turning to Allen.

"There will be but one course possible, sir, if such an insult be offered to the freemen of Annapolis. We would follow the example of Boston patriots and destroy the tea," Allen promptly answered, his face flushing at the thought that Maryland's rights should be lightly considered.

"Mistress Crowningshield, it is plainly to be seen that you are to be congratulated on your nephew as well as your niece," said Mr. Purriance as the two visitors rose to take their departure.

"Why, indeed, I think you are right, sir," responded Mrs. Crowningshield with a graceful curtsy, that made Barbara Anne resolve to make every endeavor to imitate it.

After the visitors had departed, Allen again spoke of Mr. Stewart's ship.

"The *Peggy Stewart* will never be permitted to land contraband goods. We will never submit to such an invasion of our liberties," he declared.

"But Allen, how can you stop it?" asked Barbara Anne.

Allen shook his head. "I'm not sure. 'Twould be only fair to destroy the ship," he declared.

But Aunt Crowningshield shook her head at this; like many others she dreaded any act of violence that would promptly lead to a declaration of war between England and the thirteen American Colonies.

Martin was waiting with the two horses in front of the house at an early hour the next morning, and Mrs. Crowningshield and Barbara Anne went to the porch to bid Allen good-bye, and Allen found a moment to whisper:

"Good news, Bab! You'll be home in a week!" but before Barbara Anne could ask him a question, he had run down the steps, swung himself into the saddle, and with a wave of his hand, was galloping down the street.

Barbara Anne gazed after him wonderingly. "Home in a week," she repeated to herself, and was just deciding that she had misunderstood her brother's words when Aunt Crowningshield put her arm about the little girl and said:

"I have promised Allen to visit Annapolis; and that you and I will start a week from to-day; and I believe we will journey by packet. 'Tis much the easier way, and the outlaws are becoming less troublesome, so I think we will travel safely."

CHAPTER XX

It was evident that Aunt Crowningshield was well pleased at the thought of her proposed journey to Annapolis; and as the days passed, more rapidly than Barbara Anne would have believed possible, Mrs. Crowningshield asked many questions about Amy, and declared that she looked forward to making the acquaintance of a little girl with so brave a spirit.

Barbara Anne no longer dreaded the sewing hour, for she was eager to finish the two muslin aprons that she might take them home as a present for Amy. Aunt Crowningshield often sat with her little niece in the cool drawing-room for this hour, and Barbara Anne admired the fine embroidery over which her aunt busied herself, and began to wish that she, too, could set such perfect stitches; and when Mrs. Crowningshield suggested that, after they reached Annapolis, she should teach Barbara Anne to draw designs of leaf and spray, buds and blossoms, to embroider on lawn and cambric, the little girl was at once eager to begin.

"It is a useful art," said Mrs. Crowningshield, and one that queens have not disdained to practise.

Queen Mary of Scotland found comfort in such work
when her cousin Elizabeth of England shut her up in
lonely prisons."

And in reply to Barbara Anne's questions her aunt
told her the story of Mary of Scotland, who came to
Edinborough from France as a young girl, and
whose beauty and charm won all hearts; and then of
wars and unhappiness and imprisonment.

Barbara Anne listened thoughtfully. It seemed to
her that kings and queens were very unfortunate
people; and Aunt Crowningshield agreed with her.

"They are indeed, my dear, and worse. They are
silly; because it is, at best, a make-believe. It will be a
proud day when Americans declare themselves a free
nation, and when no far-off king can reign over us."

Dor-dor was now permitted to run about the
house, and showed such an evident attachment
toward Mrs. Crowningshield that she declared she
would indeed be sorry to give him up.

"Perhaps you like the other puppy even better
than Dor-dor?" she said to Barbara Anne; but
Barbara Anne shook her head.

"No, I like Dor-dor best," she replied soberly, for
she quickly realized that Aunt Crowningshield
would be greatly pleased if Barbara Anne should
give her the puppy.

"I can't," Barbara Anne assured herself. "Of
course I can't," but this decision did not satisfy her.

She recalled that she had refused to give Doris one of the puppies. "If I wouldn't give Doris one, of course I can't give Dor-dor to Aunt Crowningshield," she thought, and reminded herself that Allen had given them to her. Nevertheless, she began to wish that she had never thought of bringing the puppy to Baltimore; for before the end of the week Dor-dor had entirely deserted the little girl, following Mrs. Crowningshield wherever she went and howling dismally if she was out of his sight.

The day of their sail down Chesapeake Bay to Annapolis dawned fair and clear. There was a favorable wind; and the large sloop, that was called a "packet," on which Mrs. Crowningshield and Barbara Anne had taken passage, skimmed over the blue waters, and Barbara Anne promptly decided it was a much pleasanter way to travel than on horseback. Milly, the negro maid, was with them; and Dor-dor, happily curled up at Mrs. Crowningshield's feet, no longer made any pretense of interest in Barbara Anne.

Mrs. Crowningshield was as eager for the first glimpse of Annapolis as was Barbara Anne; and the little girl began to feel that, after all, Great-Aunt Crowningshield was not to be greatly feared.

When the big sloop drew in at the wharf at Annapolis Barbara Anne could see that her father and mother and Allen were there to welcome the travelers. Although the little girl had not been away two weeks, it was her first absence from home, and when she stepped on shore and ran to meet her mother she was sure that the best part of any visit was the coming home.

The September days passed quickly, and Great-Aunt Crowningshield seemed to grow younger with each week. Now that she was a visitor with no responsibility in regard to her young nieces the girls found her a charming companion, and liked nothing better than to have Aunt Barbara Anne show them the proper way to dance a minuet, to play for them on Elinor's guitar, or perhaps to sit quietly beside her on the terrace and watch her slender white hands deftly shaping the delicate embroideries in which she was so skilled.

Barbara Anne and Doris soon became her pupils in this art, and vied with each other as to which could do the best work; and Amy Fletcher also became her pupil. Mrs. Crowningshield delighted in Amy's clever drawings of trailing vines, and declared that the little girl was an artist.

Mrs. Crowningshield had much to say of Colonel George Washington, of Virginia, and declared that when the Continental forces should unite as an American army, which they did early in the following year, Colonel Washington should be appointed Commander-in-chief.

"Colonel Washington has military training and experience, and every high quality of character to fit him to lead us to victory," she would say; and Mr. Browne agreed with this, although he still hoped that the King might repent of his unjust treatment of the Colonies, and their rights established without warfare.

It was several weeks after Barbara Anne's return from Baltimore before she saw Peggy Stewart, for since Peggy's selfish behavior on the day of the runaway drive, both Doris and Barbara Anne had avoided Peggy. They no longer went to see her or included her in their invitations for the garden-parties or picnics that their mother so often planned for them.

But one day early in October when Barbara Anne and Rissie were on their way to the Fletchers' cabin and had turned down Hanover Street, Peggy came down the steps of her father's house and stood directly in front of them.

"I s'pose you are going to visit Miss Amy Fletcher," she said scornfully, for although Peggy was not yet eight years old, she really believed that a girl who lived in a shabby cabin could not be worth visiting.

"Yes, Amy is my best friend; and my Aunt Crowningshield says she is an artist," responded Barbara Anne, as she endeavored to make her way past Peggy, for she had no wish to renew their former friendship.

"An 'artist'? I s'pose that means a rebel, for my father says that Fletcher is a rebel against his King!" declared Peggy.

"Don' yo' talk back, Miss Bar'b'y Anne. Don' yo', now! 'Member wot yo' ma tole yo' nebber to argify," cautioned Rissie. "Ladies nebber argify," she declared, shaking her head warningly; and Barbara Anne managed to slip past Peggy without speaking.

But she was not to escape so easily, for Peggy called after her:

"You are no better than a rebel yourself, Barbara Anne Browne. My father says that all Annapolis is talking of the way you hid messages from an English officer."

At this Barbara Anne turned quickly, and quite forgetting Rissie's warning not to "argify," called back:

"I'm glad I did."

"I don't like you, Barbara Anne Browne," shouted Peggy angrily. "My father's ship is bringing me————"

But Barbara Anne did not wait to hear Peggy finish her sentence; she began to run and Rissie kept pace with her, and when they were out of hearing of Peggy's angry voice Barbara Anne smiled at Rissie and said:

"Peggy is always talking about that old ship that's named after her, and the fine things it brings from France and England, but I don't see that they do her much good."

Rissie was too much out of breath to reply.

"Don' yo' be quarrelin' wid lille gals," she finally managed to say, and Barbara Anne clung to Rissie's arm and laughed, and promised Rissie that she would not quarrel with anyone.

"I hears yo' great-aunt a-sayin' she done mean ter staht home 'til dat ship *Peggy Stewart* come into port," said Rissie soberly. "Yo' great-aunt say she reckon de *Peggy Stewart* a-gwine ter fetch a cargo dat'll set Marylan' fo'ks ablaze! Mus' be sum kin' o' torches?" and Rissie looked questioningly at her young mistress.

"It's tea, Rissie!" Barbara Anne whispered, and Rissie's hands were raised in horror. She well knew with what opposition Maryland people would regard such a cargo, and now understood what Mistress Crowningshield meant.

Amy and her mother gave Barbara Anne a warm welcome, and when Barbara Anne told of her encounter with Peggy Stewart Amy shook her head solemnly.

"Poor Peggy," she said softly, thinking how unfortunate the little Tory girl must be to be always so ready to quarrel.

"It shu'ly do beat all," whispered Rissie, as she watched the two girls. To-day they were busy with drawing embroidery patterns with which to surprise Great-Aunt Crowningshield, and the puzzled Rissie wondered to herself as she listened to Amy's gay laughter and noticed that Barbara Anne smiled happily as she bent over the little table.

"I reckon it's kin' of a gif' ter be happy," Rissie decided, remembering Peggy Stewart's angry words and discontented expression.

CHAPTER XXI

MR. CHARLES CARROLL

It was not only little Peggy Stewart and Barbara Anne's great-aunt who were eager for the arrival of Mr. Anthony Stewart's square-sterned brig, the *Peggy Stewart*, that had sailed from London on July 23, 1774, and was due to reach Annapolis in early October. The citizens were all on the outlook for a sight of the brig, and days before her arrival there were many rumors as to her cargo.

Barbara Anne and Doris were sure that the brig must be chiefly loaded with dolls from Paris, silk dresses and fine shoes and stockings for Peggy; the possibility that Mr. Stewart meant to smuggle tea into the province against the known determination of the citizens was only a vague rumor, but created much excitement.

"I'll be off for home as soon as I know the *Peggy*'s cargo," said Great-Aunt Crowningshield, patting Dor-dor's rough head, and smiling at Barbara Anne, as they stood together on the terrace looking off toward the harbor where a brig was just coming to anchor. Allen had been watching the vessel through his spy-glass; and, on making sure it was the long-watched-for *Peggy Stewart*, had raced off toward the wharves.

"But why do you not stay and live with us, Aunt Crowningshield?" Barbara Anne said, thinking to herself that this smiling, friendly person was very different from the one she had so dreaded visiting.

But Aunt Crowningshield shook her head. "My visit has been overlong, and I am needed at home," she said, "but I would like well if you would go home with me; but I will not ask you now, dear child, for the time is near when America must defend itself, and war begin; and you should be at home."

Mrs. Crowningshield's voice was so grave and her expression so serious that Barbara Anne's smile vanished. She began to feel sorry for Aunt Crowningshield, who had no little girls of her own to keep her company in the big house in Baltimore, and who must even leave Dor-dor behind her on leaving Annapolis. And Barbara Anne made a sudden resolve: Dor-dor should go to Baltimore with Great-Aunt Barbara Anne.

"Aunt Crowningshield, I'm going to give Dor-dor to you. He'll be company for you," she said quickly, and then added, "And he likes you much better than he does anyone else; and, you see, Doris and I have Barbar, and Oric has left Pounce for us to take care of."

"Why, Barbara Anne, I would not have ventured to ask for Dor-dor, but there is no gift I would value more," said Mistress Crowningshield, thinking to herself that her little namesake was the most generous girl in all Maryland; and that on her return to Baltimore she would send her her own saddle-horse to make up for the loss of the puppy.

"Let us walk toward the wharves and get news of the *Peggy's* cargo," suggested Mrs. Crowningshield; and hand-in-hand the white-haired woman and the little girl walked down the pleasant road to the harbor; and soon met groups of excited men and heard that the *Peggy Stewart* had seventeen packages of tea among her cargo, and that Mr. Stewart had already paid the duties thereon.

" 'Tis an insult to the people of this province that he should do such a thing," they heard one man declare, while another said that there should be a meeting of citizens to take action upon this open defiance of the wishes of Maryland people.

Allen soon joined his aunt and sister, and told them a committee had been appointed to guard the vessel and prevent the landing of the tea.

"Will it be sent back to England?" asked Barbara Anne, "and will not Peggy get all the sweets and toys that are on board for her?"

"Who knows?" Allen replied. "Mr. Stewart is already alarmed as to what may happen, and declares himself ready to comply with whatever the citizens ask. He fears for his own safety."

As they walked slowly toward home and Allen gave his aunt the story of the discovery of the tea, Barbara Anne's thoughts centered on Peggy, and she no longer felt angry toward the little girl. As they drew near the Stewart mansion on Hanover Street she stopped and said:

"I think I would like to see Peggy."

Allen gazed at her in amazement, and was about to say that it was not the time for a loyal American girl to visit a Tory maid, but before he could speak Aunt Crowningshield had nodded approvingly.

"I will tell Rissie to come for you in an hour, my dear," she said, and Barbara Anne started up the steps. Before she could lift the heavy knocker the door opened and Barbara Anne found herself face to face with Mr. Anthony Stewart. His face was grave and troubled, and he looked down at her frowningly.

"If you please, sir, I am Barbara Anne Browne, and I have come to see Peggy," and Barbara Anne curtsied, and stood awaiting a word of welcome.

For a moment she thought Mr. Stewart had not heard her, then he motioned her to step inside, and Barbara Anne found herself standing in the hall and heard the big door close behind her as Mr. Stewart disappeared.

For a few moments Barbara Anne stood looking about and expecting a servant or Peggy herself to appear. But the house was very quiet, and Barbara

Anne began to wonder why Mr. Stewart had bade her enter. She was just deciding to start for home when Peggy appeared on the stairs, and stood looking down at her.

"Barbara! Oh, Barbara Anne! Will you go with me? I am to carry a message to Mr. Carroll. I am to go in my pony-cart. Father said no one would imagine I was carrying a message," said Peggy, talking as fast as possible, and evidently quite forgetting her dislike toward her former friend.

"It is to ask Mr. Carroll's help," pleaded Peggy. "My father says there is no knowing what the rebels may do!"

"Mr. Carroll is not a Tory," replied Barbara.

"Of course he isn't; but my father says he is a just man and will see fair play. I like not to go alone," and the pleading note in the little girl's voice made Barbara Anne speak more kindly. She began to wonder why she had stopped at Peggy's door. But this half-frightened little girl asking her help did not seem the selfish, exacting Peggy who had thrust Barbara Anne from the pony-cart on that unfortunate runaway; and now Barbara Anne soberly agreed to Peggy's pleading to accompany her to Carrollton.

"We must hurry," urged Peggy, and the two little girls ran through the house and found the ponies harnessed and waiting near the rear door; and before Mistress Crowningshield and Allen reached home

the two little girls were well on their way to
Carrollton with Mr. Stewart's letter asking the
advice of one of the chief citizens of Maryland. Mr.
Carroll's character as a champion upon whom
America could rely was beyond question; and his
sense of justice was so well known that Mr. Stewart
had declared himself ready to follow whatever
course Mr. Carroll might suggest in regard to the
contraband cargo of the *Peggy Stewart*.

Peggy sat very close to Barbara Anne as the
ponies trotted swiftly along; her face was tear-
stained and anxious.

"My mother is ill in bed, and my father says she
must not know of all this trouble," she told Barbara
Anne. "Do you think the rebels will do my father
harm?" she questioned, quite forgetting that she
had taunted Barbara Anne with being a rebel.

"Mr. Carroll will tell your father what to do,"
responded Barbara Anne, and remembering the
muttered threats against "Tory Stewart" of the
crowd at the wharf, she realized that Peggy was
bound on an important mission.

As the ponies reached Carrollton, Mr. Carroll was
just mounting his horse to ride to Annapolis.
Recognizing the two little girls he came toward the
pony-cart and greeted them smilingly, and took the
letter that Peggy gave him with a faltering explanation of her father's wish for Mr. Carroll's advice.

Mr. Carroll read the letter quickly. He already knew of the arrival of the tea-laden brig, and Mr. Stewart's readiness in paying the tax on the obnoxious cargo was an offence to American liberties, and he knew that Peggy's father might well fear for his personal safety.

"I am just starting for Annapolis but I may not see your father; and I have not time to write a response to his letter, but you can take him my opinion," and Mr. Carroll regarded the two little girls questioningly.

"Yes, sir! I am quite sure I can remember any message for my father!" Peggy replied, and Mr. Carroll nodded approvingly.

"Tell him this: It is not enough for him to ship the tea back to London. And whatever may be my wish to prevent violence it will not be in my power to protect Mr. Stewart unless he publicly confesses his fault, and sets fire to his ship and its unlawful cargo."

"Oh!" gasped Peggy, and Barbara Anne's brown eyes widened in terror at the thought of a burning ship. For the moment both the little girls quite forgot Peggy's long expected toys, and thought only of Mr. Stewart's danger.

"Drive back and tell your father at once," said Mr. Carroll.

Barbara Anne had not spoken a word. This drive began to seem even a greater adventure than her

encounter with the English soldiers on her ride to
Baltimore; and this thought had but flashed
through her mind when Mr. Carroll spoke to her.

"Did you come to protect little Peggy?" he questioned, and before Barbara Anne could reply continued, "I think you are the little maid who saved our
messages to loyal men in Baltimore."

When Barbara Anne flushed and said: "I was with
my brother Allen, sir," Mr. Carroll quickly answered:

"Your brother is duly proud of you, I doubt not;
and so are the loyal men of Annapolis. But I must
not linger," and again bidding Peggy to carefully
remember his message to her father, he bade them
good-bye and was off, his swift horse speeding
down the avenue followed by his well-mounted
negro servant.

And now the ponies' heads were turned toward
home. Peggy could no longer keep back her tears. To
carry Mr. Carroll's message to her father to burn the
fine ship that had been named for her seemed
almost more than the little girl was equal to, and
when they reached Hanover Street she exclaimed:

"Oh, Barbara Anne! I do not think Mr. Carroll
really meant for my father to burn the ship. I will
tell him that Mr. Carroll bids him tell the people of
Annapolis that he meant no harm, and that he asks
forgiveness. It will be dreadful to burn the ship."

There was no time for Barbara Anne to reply. The ponies had been halted in front of the Stewart mansion, and Mr. Anthony Stewart came hurrying to meet them, and anxiously questioned Peggy as to Mr. Carroll's response to his letter.

"Oh, Father! He said—he said—you must—must ask pardon of the citizens, and—and—and——" Peggy could not finish the message. She was only a child; and she now leaned against Barbara Anne and began to cry.

Mr. Stewart lifted his little daughter from the pony-cart and endeavored to comfort her, but his face was troubled.

"I should have gone myself," he said with a little sigh. "It was a pity to send Peggy on so serious an errand."

"If you please, sir, I remember exactly what Mr. Carroll said. He bade Peggy tell you that he would not answer for your safety unless you publicly confessed your fault and set fire to the *Peggy Stewart* and her cargo," repeated Barbara Anne.

"Burn the *Peggy Stewart!*" exclaimed Mr. Stewart, who had already heard the threat that "The Tory should be tarred and feathered," and knew himself to be in serious danger.

"I think I must go home now. Good-bye, Peggy," said Barbara Anne, as Rissie came down from the porch where she had awaited the return of her young mistress.

Mr. Stewart had started toward the house with Peggy, but troubled and alarmed as he was by the results of his insult to the liberties of America, he quickly remembered that Barbara Anne had not only done him an important service but that she had also proven her friendliness toward his little daughter. He now turned quickly and said:

"I thank you, Barbara Anne, for so clearly remembering Mr. Carroll's message. You have done me a great service, and you shall be the first to know that I will fulfill Mr. Carroll's advice to the letter. I will acknowledge my fault, and will burn the *Peggy Stewart* at whatever time and place the citizens of Annapolis may appoint."

"Thank you, Mr. Stewart," said Barbara Anne, as she curtsied to this kindly man whose only offence was his loyalty to the English government.

Rissie now drew Barbara Anne toward home, muttering wrathfully over her long wait for her young mistress. But Barbara Anne was hardly conscious of what Rissie was saying. She was eager to reach home and tell Allen the wonderful news. She ran up the steps to the terrace and into the house and called: "Allen! Allen!" but it was Aunt Crowningshield, with Dor-dor at her heels, who was the first to appear in the sitting-room where Barbara Anne again called,

"Doris! Elinor!" and in a moment both the girls, closely followed by Mrs. Browne and Allen, hurried into the room.

"What is it, my dear child? What has happened?" Mrs. Browne asked as she noticed Barbara Anne's flushed face and heard her excited voice.

"It's about the *Peggy Stewart*. The ship and the tea are to be burned. Mr. Stewart says so," declared Barbara.

CHAPTER XXII

THE BURNING OF THE "PEGGY"

"WELL, the destruction of tea in Boston harbor was a bold act, but this tea-burning at Annapolis far surpasses it," declared Aunt Crowningshield, a few days after Barbara Anne's announcement. For Mr. Anthony Stewart had fulfilled his promise, and the *Peggy Stewart*, on the morning of Monday, October 17, 1774, was run aground near Windmill Point, not far from the very ledge where Barbara Anne had first seen Fletcher and his companions, and Mr. Stewart had himself lighted the flames, and in a few hours the brig, with her cargo, sails, and cordage was in a blaze and burned to the water's edge.

Crowds of people gathered to watch the destruction of the Tory ship. It was a great day in the history of Maryland, for its patriotic citizens had taken their stand. Their liberties had been openly invaded, and they promptly resisted the wrong.

The entire Browne household, accompanied by Amy Fletcher and her father, had watched the flames devour the ship; and Barbara Anne's thoughts centered about Peggy, and she hoped the little girl might not see or know what had befallen the brig that had in times past brought her so many treasures.

Barbara Anne no longer remembered Peggy's selfishness and her fretful complaints, or recalled them only to make excuses for Peggy. The two little girls never met again after their ride to Carrollton. Mr. Stewart's sympathies were not with the American cause, and he soon found it advisable to remove his family to New York and later on to New Brunswick. That he remembered the service Barbara Anne had rendered him in delivering Mr. Carroll's message was proven when, on the departure of the family, Peggy's gray ponies and cart were sent to Barbara Anne with a friendly note from Mr. Stewart asking her to accept them as a gift from his little daughter.

Barbara Anne soon learned to drive the ponies herself, and, with Amy beside her, drove about the pleasant roads, and often declared that the ponies were as much Amy's as they were her own. Whenever Barbara Anne said this, the little crippled girl would smile radiantly and be very sure that she was the most fortunate girl in all Maryland.

On the day after the burning of the *Peggy Stewart*, Mistress Crowningshield and Dor-dor had taken passage for Baltimore. But none of her nieces would ever again dread a visit to their great-aunt. They had discovered that she could be kind and generous, and that no one could make as fine a curtsy or dance the minuet more gracefully than Great-Aunt Barbara Anne.

And Mistress Crowningshield had discovered that too many lesson hours were not needed to learn the many things that she could teach, for she realized that Barbara Anne watched her closely and endeavored to imitate her; and Great-Aunt Barbara Anne smiled approvingly, thinking to herself that Barbara Anne would learn many things without lessons.

She often told the story of Barbara Anne's encounter with the British officer, and the way in which the little girl had defeated his plans, and would end the tale by saying:

"This girl is a little maid of Maryland, and my namesake."

Other Stories in this Series are:

A LITTLE MAID OF MASSACHUSETTS COLONY

A LITTLE MAID OF OLD NEW YORK

A LITTLE MAID OF OLD PHILADELPHIA

A LITTLE MAID OF OLD CONNECTICUT

A LITTLE MAID OF TICONDEROGA

A LITTLE MAID OF PROVINCETOWN